THE SLICK STRATEGY

A Unique Profitable Options Trading Method

Unlock Weekly Gains with Little Capital, Risk, Effort, and Market Expertise

Paul Caselli

Paperback ISBN: 978-3-31056-099-0
Hardback ISBN: 978-3-03680-644-0

Legal Notice

This book is only for personal use. No part of this publication may
be reproduced, distributed, or transmitted in any form or by any
means without the author's explicit permission. Unauthorized
use is strictly prohibited and may result in legal action.

Disclaimer Notice

The information provided in this book is for entertainment purposes
only. While every effort has been made to ensure that the content is
accurate, up-to-date, and reliable, no warranties of any kind, express or
implied, are made. The author makes no representations as to the accuracy
or completeness of the information contained within this book.

Readers acknowledge that the author is not a licensed legal, financial,
or professional advisor. The content of this book has been derived from
various sources and is intended to provide general information only.
It should not be used as a substitute for professional advice. Before
attempting any techniques, strategies, or actions presented in this book,
please consult a licensed professional. This is not financial advice.

By reading this notice and continuing to use the information provided
in this book, the reader agrees that under no circumstances will the
author be held liable for any losses or damages, direct or indirect, that
may result from the use of the information contained herein, including,
but not limited to, errors, omissions, or inaccuracies. Readers assume full
responsibility for any consequences arising from their use of the content.

Contents

Preamble

I understand that encountering a highly profitable options strategy that needs as little as $3,000, involves minimal risk, demands only basic stock market knowledge, and requires very little time and effort, might sound too good to be true. However, if you take the time to read the following chapters, you'll quickly grasp the simplicity of the Slick Strategy, its incredible profit potential, the limited effort required, and how it can be easily tailored to fit your investment capacity and risk tolerance, leading you to achieve financial independence now.

Let me begin by sharing my personal journey.

Unlike many investment stories, I didn't have to lose a fortune before learning how to make money. I'm not a genius; I was simply cautious, naturally risk-averse, and had a bit of luck. When I bought my first stock, I knew little about investing. In 2018, I began investing in stocks through my bank, which handled most of the investment decisions. However, I wasn't very satisfied with this approach. So, toward the end of 2018, when my investment returns were nearly flat, I switched to an online broker that caters to retail investors like me. I did not really have an investment strategy, but fortunately, it was 2019, a very bullish year when it was not that difficult to make money. By the end of that year, I had indeed made a few thousand dollars. However, I knew this success was due more to favourable market conditions than my expertise. I also knew that investing was crucial for building my wealth, but I felt uncomfortable remaining invested without a proper strategy. I was afraid I could lose the money I made if I didn't know exactly what to do. So, in January 2020, I stepped out of the market to reflect on my investment approach before making any further moves with real money. I knew I had been lucky until then, but I also knew that luck could run out at any moment. I needed a proper investment strategy to give me confidence in what I was doing so I could sleep well at night.

Disinvesting at that moment turned out to be perfect timing, as the market crashed one month later due to the COVID-19 pandemic. However, the market's V-shaped recovery in June 2020 made me eager to re-enter. Despite making good money by the end of the year, I couldn't shake the unease of not knowing if I was making the right decisions. I lacked the confidence that comes from being sure about your choices. My success seemed attributable to good market conditions and luck, which I knew wouldn't last forever. So, at the beginning of 2021, I stepped out of the market again. This turned out to be another fortunate decision, as most of the stocks I was invested in started declining, culminating in a painful crash in 2022.

So, I was back to where I started at the beginning of 2020. I then decided that instead of focusing on what *I didn't know*, I should focus on what *I did know*. From the outset, I knew that following the hype and buying popular stocks wasn't for me. I feared excessive valuations driven by crowd euphoria rather than actual earnings. The idea of my stock losing 50% of its value due to changing market sentiment kept me up at night. Naturally, I considered the value investing approach, but I had little appeal for long-term investments. I didn't want to wait 10, 15, or even 20 years to see profits. I wasn't aiming to become a billionaire like Warren Buffet. I simply wanted to reasonably increase my earnings and achieve financial independence as soon as possible. Besides, I lacked the knowledge and expertise to effectively pursue value investing. I didn't understand balance sheets, cash flows, and valuations very well, and relying on expert advice was too expensive for my limited capital. A friend suggested trading, but I quickly realized I didn't possess the technical analysis skills needed for effective daily trading. More importantly, I couldn't handle the huge volatility and constant shifts from losses to gains. I didn't want such a stressful life.

Ultimately, I simply wanted a steady and reliable stream of income each month, just a few extra thousand dollars to complement my salary and enable me to save more and enjoy life with minimal effort and risk.

Then, while reading an article on MarketWatch.com, I came across a mention of Warren Buffett using options to buy stocks at desired prices and recommending options trading for portfolio protection and extra income. This piqued my interest. I began collecting all sorts of information about option trading: books, magazines, online articles and YouTube videos. By the beginning of 2022, after almost a year of deep immersion and some trial and error, I couldn't call myself an expert out of respect for professionals in the field, but I was certainly very knowledgeable. I understood the main options strategies, from basic covered calls to more sophisticated ones like iron condors and butterfly spreads.

Initially, I struggled to find an option strategy that suited me. Covered calls were easy to implement and low-risk but required significant capital to generate a good income. The Wheel strategy required even more capital and skills to select the right stocks for long-term investment, which I lacked. More complicated strategies often required predicting market movements, which I couldn't do. The risk/reward ratio was often not worth it. Making $1,000 from a trade where I could risk losing ten or twenty times more wasn't for me. Meanwhile, other strategies required constant monitoring, which I didn't like either.

However, during the summer of 2022, after extensive testing that began in early 2021, I finally completed the design of a strategy that worked for me. I must admit that it wasn't perfect from the beginning; I had to adjust it, make modifications, and learn from my mistakes. I backtested the strategy using 10 years of market data and historical charts to confirm my assumptions, and then verified everything with AI support. Data shows that the strategy is successful on average more than 88% of the time. If executed properly and consistently, it is profitable month after month. For the past two years, I've been implementing this strategy, and now I can say in full confidence that it works!

In the coming chapters, I'll explain this weekly options trading strategy, which relies on statistical data. It requires little market expertise, balance sheet study, or technical analysis skills. All you need to start is $3000, with only $700 at risk. The strategy requires no more than one hour per week and can generate, on average, a minimum of $750 per month. With an investment of $10,000, as I am currently doing, it can generate an average monthly income of approximately $6,000, with a maximum risk capital of around $7,000.

I decided to write this book to help others who, like me, are struggling to find their way to financial independence. This book has no filler; it goes straight to the core and delivers on its promises. If you're looking for a reliable stream of monthly income, to build wealth rapidly despite limited stock market expertise, a low risk appetite, limited capital, and scarce time, the **Slick Strategy** is for you. The coming chapters, along with a step-by-step video guide, will provide all the information needed to master its implementation and see your account grow week by week.

1. Options

Options are versatile financial instruments that derive their value from an underlying asset, such as a stock, bond, commodity, or index. As derivatives, their price movements are based on the price movements of the underlying financial instrument. This book does not aim to detail how options work but rather to explain a unique strategy using options. If you are already familiar with options, particularly index options, and understand how they work, you can skip this chapter and proceed to the next. Otherwise, you will find a summary of the options' characteristics below. For a deeper understanding of options, I recommend *Options Trading for Dummies*.

However, to understand and apply the Slick Strategy, no specialised knowledge or expertise in options trading is required. The detailed explanations in the upcoming Chapter 2 will be more than sufficient for you to start your journey towards financial independence. The following paragraphs are only intended to provide you with a basic understanding of the different types of options and their main characteristics, enabling you to easily comprehend the key advantages offered by this financial tool and its use through the Slick strategy.

1.1 Options characteristics

An option contract provides the holder with the right, but not the obligation, to buy or sell the underlying asset at a predetermined price, known as the strike price, within a specific period. This flexibility allows investors to leverage their positions, hedge against potential losses, and enhance their portfolios through various strategic approaches.

The main characteristics of options include:

- **Strike Price:** The price at which the option can be exercised.
- **Expiration Date:** The last date on which the option can be exercised.
- **Premium:** The cost of purchasing the option.

Options are primarily classified into two types: call options and put options. A call option contract gives the holder the right to purchase the underlying asset at the strike price, whereas a put option contract grants the holder the right to sell the underlying asset at the strike price. These rights are not obligations, which means the holder can choose whether or not to exercise the option contract based on the prevailing market conditions. The seller, or writer, of the option contract, on the other hand, is obligated to fulfil the contract if the holder decides to exercise their right.

In the context of options trading, *"in the money"* (ITM) and *"out of the money"* (OTM) refer to whether exercising an option would be profitable or not.

In the Money (ITM)

- **Call Option**: A call option is in the money if the current price of the underlying asset is higher than the option's strike price. For example, if you have a call option with a strike price of $50 and the underlying asset is trading at $60, the option is in the money by $10.
- **Put Option**: A put option is in the money if the current price of the underlying asset is lower than the option's strike price. For example, if you have a put option with a strike price of $50 and the underlying asset is trading at $40, the option is in the money by $10.

Out of the Money (OTM)

- **Call Option**: A call option is out of the money if the current price of the underlying asset is lower than the option's strike price. For example, if you have a call option with a strike price of $50 and the underlying asset is trading at $40, the option is out of the money.
- **Put Option**: A put option is out of the money if the current price of the underlying asset is higher than the option's strike price. For example, if you have a put option with a strike price of $50 and the underlying asset is trading at $60, the option is out of the money.

At the Money (ATM)

As an additional term, an option is **at the money (ATM)** when the current price of the underlying asset is equal to the option's strike price.

Understanding whether an option is ITM or OTM is crucial for traders as it affects the option's intrinsic value and potential profitability.

Each option contract typically represents 100 shares of the underlying stock. This standardization allows for more manageable trading and uniformity in the options market.

One of the key features of options is their expiration date, which defines the time frame within which the option can be exercised. Options can be either American-style or European-style. American-style options can be exercised at any point up until the expiration date, providing more flexibility for the holder. European-style options, however, can only be exercised on the expiration date itself. This distinction influences the strategies and risk management practices employed by investors.

The price of an option, known as the premium, is influenced by several factors, including the current price of the underlying asset, the strike price, the time remaining until expiration, and the volatility of the underlying asset. Higher volatility increases the potential for significant price movements, thus raising the premium. Conversely, a longer time until expiration also generally results in a higher premium due to the increased likelihood of the option becoming profitable.

Options can be traded on various exchanges, such as the Chicago Board Options Exchange (CBOE) or over-the-counter (OTC) between private parties. Exchange-traded options are standardized in terms of contract size, expiration dates, and strike prices, which enhances liquidity and transparency. In contrast, OTC options can be customized to meet the specific needs of the parties involved, offering more flexibility but with less liquidity and greater counterparty risk.

Investors utilize options for various purposes, including speculation, hedging, and income generation. Traders aim to profit from the price movements of the underlying asset by buying or selling options based on their market outlook. Hedgers use options to protect their existing positions from adverse price movements, effectively transferring risk to other market participants. Income generation strategies often involve writing options to collect premiums, providing an additional revenue stream.

The versatility and complexity of options make them a powerful tool in the financial markets. In general, as the financial landscape evolves, options continue to play a crucial role in the toolkit of sophisticated investors, offering opportunities for innovation and growth in portfolio management.

1.2 Call Options

A call option is a financial contract that grants the holder the right, but not the obligation, to purchase a specified quantity of an underlying asset at a predetermined price, known as the strike price, within a defined time frame. This feature provides investors with significant leverage, as they can control a substantial amount of the underlying asset for a fraction of the price. Call options are widely used by investors seeking to capitalize on the potential rise in the price of the underlying asset without committing large amounts of capital upfront.

The mechanics of a call option are straightforward. When an investor buys a call option, they pay a premium to the seller or writer of the option contract. This premium represents the cost of acquiring the right to purchase the underlying asset at the strike price. The value of the call option contract, or its premium, is influenced by several factors, including the current price of the underlying asset, the strike price, the time remaining until expiration, and the volatility of the underlying asset. Higher volatility generally increases the premium, as it raises the likelihood of significant price movements that could make the option contract more valuable.

To understand the potential benefits and risks of call options, consider an example involving a stock. Suppose an investor believes that the stock of Company XYZ, currently trading at $100 per share, will increase in value over the next three months. The investor could purchase a call option with a strike price of $105, expiring in three months, for a premium of $5 per share. If the stock price rises to $120 before the option expires, the investor can exercise the option, buying the stock at $105 and potentially selling it at the market price of $120, thus realizing a profit of $15 per share minus the $5 premium paid, resulting in a net gain of $10 per share.

However, if the stock price remains below $105, the investor would likely choose not to exercise the option, as it would not be profitable. In this case, the investor's loss is limited to the premium paid, which is a key advantage of call options—they allow for leveraged gains while capping potential losses at the initial investment (the premium). This limited risk is one of the main attractions of call options for investors looking to speculate on upward price movements.

In summary, call options are powerful financial instruments that provide investors with the ability to leverage their positions and speculate on the upward movement of underlying assets with limited risk. They are an integral part of various trading strategies and portfolio management techniques, offering flexibility and potential for enhanced returns.

1.3 Put Options

A put option is a financial contract that, contrary to the call options, gives the holder the right, but not the obligation, to sell a specified quantity of an underlying asset at a predetermined price, known as the strike price, within a set time frame. Put options are valuable tools for investors who anticipate a decline in the price of the underlying asset, as they provide the opportunity to profit from such a downward movement without actually holding the asset. They are also essential for hedging strategies, allowing investors to protect their portfolios against potential losses.

The mechanics of a put option involve the holder paying a premium to the seller or writer of the option in exchange for the right to sell the underlying asset at the strike price. The value of the put option, or its premium, is influenced by several factors, including the current price of the underlying asset, the strike price, the time remaining until expiration, and the volatility of the underlying asset. Generally, higher volatility increases the premium, as it raises the likelihood of significant price movements that could make the option more valuable.

To illustrate the potential benefits and risks of put options, consider an example involving a stock. Suppose an investor believes that the stock of Company ABC, currently trading at $50 per share, will decrease in value over the next two months. The investor could purchase a put option contract with a strike price of $45, expiring in two months, for a premium of $2 per share. If the stock price falls to $35 before the option expires, the investor can exercise the option contract, selling the stock at $45 and potentially buying it back at the market price of $35, thus realizing a profit of $10 per share minus the $2 premium paid, resulting in a net gain of $8 per share.

Conversely, if the stock price remains above $45, the investor would likely choose not to exercise the option contract, as it would not be profitable. In this case, the investor's loss is limited to the premium paid, which is a key advantage of put options—they allow for leveraged gains while capping potential losses at the initial investment (the premium). This limited risk makes put options an attractive choice for investors looking to speculate on downward price movements.

Put options are also fundamental components of various trading strategies and risk management practices. For instance, a protective put strategy involves holding a long position in the underlying asset while simultaneously buying a put option on the same asset. This strategy serves as an insurance policy, protecting the investor against potential losses if the price of the underlying asset declines. The cost of this protection is the premium paid for the put option, which can be offset by the security it provides.

In summary, put options are versatile financial instruments that provide investors with the ability to hedge against potential losses and profit from declines in the prices of underlying assets. They play a crucial role in various trading strategies and risk management techniques, offering flexibility and potential for enhanced returns.

1.4 Buying and Selling Options

Options trading involves two primary actions: buying (holding) and selling (writing) options. Understanding the differences between these actions and their implications is crucial for investors aiming to utilize options effectively in their trading and investment strategies. This section will delve into the key distinctions and considerations associated with buying and selling options.

Buying Options

When an investor buys an option, they are acquiring the right, but not the obligation, to either buy (in the case of a call option) or sell (in the case of a put option) the underlying asset at the strike price before the option expires. The cost of this right is the premium paid to the option seller. Buying options is a strategy often employed by investors seeking to leverage their exposure to potential price movements of the underlying asset with limited risk.

Key Characteristics and Implications

Leverage: Buying options allows investors to control a larger position with a relatively small initial investment (the premium). This leverage can lead to substantial gains if the underlying asset's price moves favourably.

Limited Risk: The maximum loss for an option buyer is limited to the premium paid. This is a significant advantage, as it caps the potential downside, making options an attractive tool for speculative and hedging purposes.

Potential for High Returns: If the price of the underlying asset moves significantly in the desired direction (up for calls, down for puts), the returns on the option can be substantial, often exceeding the initial premium by many multiples.

Time Decay (Theta): One of the primary drawbacks of buying options is time decay. As the expiration date approaches, the value of the option erodes, especially if the price of the underlying asset remains stagnant. This means that the option must experience a favourable price movement relatively quickly to be profitable.

Selling Options

Selling, or writing, options involves creating a new option contract and selling it to an option buyer. The seller, in exchange for the premium received, takes on the obligation to buy or sell the underlying asset at the strike price if the option is exercised by the buyer. Selling options can be a strategy for generating income, but it also involves significant risk.

Key Characteristics and Implications

Income Generation: The primary motivation for selling options is to collect the premium, which can provide a steady stream of income.

This strategy is often used by investors who believe that the underlying asset's price will remain relatively stable.

Unlimited Risk for Call Sellers: For uncovered (naked) call options, the risk is theoretically unlimited because the underlying asset's price can rise indefinitely. If the buyer exercises the option, the seller must purchase the asset at the prevailing market price, potentially incurring substantial losses.

Limited Risk for Put Sellers: Selling naked put options involves the risk of the underlying asset's price falling to zero. While this is not as extreme as the risk associated with naked calls, it can still result in significant losses.

Obligation: Unlike option buyers, sellers have an obligation to fulfil the contract if the option is exercised. This obligation necessitates careful risk management and often requires maintaining a sufficient margin in the account to cover potential losses.

Profit Potential: The profit for option sellers is limited to the premium received. This contrasts with the potentially unlimited profits that buyers can achieve. The seller's strategy relies on the option expiring worthless or the price of the underlying asset moving favourably.

Time Decay (Theta): Time decay works in favour of option sellers. As the option approaches expiration, its value diminishes, benefiting the seller if the option remains out-of-the-money.

Strategic Implications and Considerations

Risk Tolerance: The choice between buying and selling options depends significantly on an investor's risk tolerance. Buyers enjoy limited risk and potential for high returns, making it suitable for those willing to accept the cost of premiums for the chance of substantial gains. Sellers, on the other hand, must be comfortable with the potentially unlimited or significant risk in exchange for limited but consistent income.

Market Outlook: Buyers typically have a directional market outlook—bullish for call options and bearish for put options. Conversely, sellers often believe that the market will remain stable or that the option will not be exercised, allowing them to profit from the premium.

Complex Strategies: Both buying and selling options can be combined into more sophisticated strategies. Such strategies can tailor risk and reward profiles to fit specific market conditions and investor goals.

In conclusion, the decision to buy or sell options involves weighing the potential for leverage and high returns against the risks and obligations associated with each action. A thorough understanding of these differences and their implications is essential for any investor looking to incorporate options into their trading strategies effectively.

Proper education, risk management, and strategic planning are crucial for harnessing the benefits of options trading while mitigating its inherent risks.

1.5 Index Options

They are derivative contracts that give the holder the right, but not the obligation, to buy or sell a specific index at a predetermined price, known as the strike price, before or at expiration. Unlike individual stock options, which are based on the value of a single stock, index options derive their value from a basket of stocks representing a specific market index, such as the S&P 500, Nasdaq 100, or Dow Jones Industrial Average. These options provide investors with a way to gain exposure to an entire market or sector, offering a broader scope of opportunities for hedging, speculation, and income generation. Index options, and more precisely those based on the S&P 500 (SPX), are the ones used for the Slick strategy.

Understanding Index Options

Structure and Types: Index options come in two primary forms: call options and put options. A call option on an index gives the holder the right to buy the index at the strike price, while a put option gives the holder the right to sell the index at the strike price. These options can be either American-style, which can be exercised at any time before expiration, or European-style, which can only be exercised at expiration. Since the SPX is a US index, American-style index options are the only ones relevant for the Slick strategy.

One of the key distinctions between index options and other types of options, such as stock options, lies in the nature of the underlying asset. Stock options are tied to individual stocks, making them susceptible to company-specific risks and events. Index options, on the other hand, represent a broad market segment, reducing the impact of individual stock volatility and offering a more diversified exposure.

Settlement: One of the distinctive features of index options is that they are cash-settled. Since an index itself is not a tangible asset, settlement occurs in cash rather than through the delivery of securities. At expiration, the difference between the strike price and the index's closing level determines the settlement amount. This cash settlement simplifies the process and avoids the complexities associated with the delivery of numerous individual stocks. For instance, if an investor holds a call option on the S&P 500 with a strike price of 4,000 and the index closes at 4,100 on expiration, the cash settlement would be the difference between the index level and the strike price (4,100 - 4,000 = 100), multiplied by the option's multiplier (typically 100). The investor would receive $10,000 (100 * 100) in cash. This contrasts with stock options, where exercising a call would result in purchasing the actual shares.

Pricing Factors: The pricing of index options is influenced by several factors, including the current level of the index, the strike price, time to expiration, interest rates, and the volatility of the index. The most commonly used model for pricing index options is the Black-Scholes model, which considers these variables to estimate the option's fair value.

Volatility plays a crucial role in pricing. Higher volatility increases the likelihood of significant price movements, raising the option's premium. Conversely, lower volatility tends to decrease the premium. This sensitivity to volatility (known as Vega) makes index options a valuable tool for investors looking to trade on market volatility.

Expiration Dates: Index options typically have monthly expiration dates, but most indices offer weekly and even daily expiration, providing traders with a wide range of expiration choices. This flexibility allows traders to tailor their strategies more precisely to their market outlook and time horizon.

Weekly index options, which are the ones used for the Slick strategy, expire the last trading day of the week, usually on Friday, unless of a National Holidays, while daily index options, often referred to as "zero-day to expiration" or "0DTE" options, expire at the end of each trading day. These short-term options are particularly attractive to active traders and institutional investors who seek to capitalize on daily market movements without holding positions overnight. The availability of these frequent expiration dates sets index options apart from many other types of options, which typically offer fewer expiration choices.

Key Considerations and Risks

Market Direction and Timing: Successful trading of index options requires accurate predictions of market direction and timing. Incorrect assumptions can lead to losses, especially given the leverage involved in options trading. Investors must carefully analyse market trends, economic indicators, and geopolitical events to inform their strategies.

Volatility Impact: Volatility significantly impacts the pricing of index options. Higher volatility increases option premiums, benefiting option sellers but posing challenges for buyers. Conversely, lower volatility reduces premiums, which can be advantageous for buyers. Understanding and anticipating changes in market volatility is crucial for effective options trading.

Time Decay (Theta): Index options are subject to time decay, meaning their value erodes as the expiration date approaches. This decay accelerates in the final weeks before expiration. Investors must manage their positions carefully to avoid significant losses due to time decay, particularly for out-of-the-money options that may expire worthless.

Liquidity and Spreads: Liquidity can vary across different index options, affecting bid-ask spreads and execution prices. Popular indexes like the S&P 500 generally offer high liquidity and narrow spreads, while less popular indexes may have wider spreads, increasing trading costs. Investors should consider liquidity when choosing index options for their strategies.

Comparing Index Options to Stock Options

Diversification: Index options offer greater diversification compared to stock options. A single index option represents exposure to a broad market segment, mitigating the impact of individual stock volatility. This diversification reduces specific risks and aligns more closely with overall market performance.

Cash Settlement vs. Physical Settlement: Index options are cash-settled, while stock options typically involve the physical delivery of shares. Cash settlement simplifies the process and reduces the administrative burden associated with handling multiple stock transactions. This feature is particularly advantageous for institutional investors and large-scale traders.

Flexibility in Expiration: The availability of multiple expiration dates, including daily expirations, provides index option traders with greater flexibility to implement short-term strategies and adjust their positions frequently. Stock options generally offer fewer expiration choices, limiting the ability to fine-tune strategies.

Impact of Corporate Events: Stock options are influenced by company-specific events such as earnings reports, mergers, and dividends. Index options, being based on a basket of stocks, are less affected by individual corporate events and more by macroeconomic factors and broad market trends.

In conclusion, index options are versatile financial instruments that offer investors a variety of opportunities for hedging, trading, and income generation. Their unique structure, cash settlement feature, and broad market exposure make them essential tools for savvy traders. By carefully considering market conditions and employing appropriate strategies such as the one proposed in this book, traders can harness the benefits of index options to enhance their portfolios and achieve their financial goals.

1.6 The Most Popular Options Strategies in Summary

Options trading offers a variety of strategies to help investors achieve different objectives, such as hedging, income generation, and speculation. Below are summaries of the most popular stock and index option strategies.

a) Covered Call

Strategy: Involves holding a long position in a stock while simultaneously selling a call option on the same stock.

Objective: Generate additional income from the premium received from selling the call option.

Application: Suitable for investors who are moderately bullish or neutral on the stock. The risk is limited to the downside of the stock position, and the upside is capped at the strike price of the sold call.

b) The wheel

Strategy: It is a systematic approach involving selling put options on a stock the investor is willing to own. If assigned, the investor buys the stock at the strike price and then sells covered call options on the owned shares.

Objective: The cycle of selling puts, acquiring the stock, and selling calls aims to generate consistent income through premiums collected from both the put and call options.

Application: The strategy leverages the investor's willingness to own the stock long-term while monetizing the options market's volatility.

c) Straddle

Strategy: Involves buying both a call and a put option on the same stock or index with the same strike price and expiration date.

Objective: Profit from significant price movements in either direction.

Application: Suitable for investors expecting high volatility but unsure of the direction. The risk is limited to the total premiums paid for the options.

d) Strangle

Strategy: Similar to a straddle, but the call and put options have different strike prices.

Objective: Profit from significant price movements in either direction with lower premiums than a straddle.

Application: Suitable for investors expecting high volatility but seeking a less expensive alternative to a straddle. The risk is limited to the total premiums paid for the options.

e) Iron Condor

Strategy: Involves selling a lower strike put, buying a lower strike put (further out of the money), selling a higher strike call, and buying a higher strike call (further out of the money).

Objective: Profit from low volatility when the price of the underlying asset remains within a specific range.

Application: Suitable for investors expecting low volatility. The maximum profit is the net premium received, and the risk is limited to the difference between the strike prices of the put or call spreads minus the net premium.

f) Butterfly Spread

Strategy: Involves buying one call (or put) at a lower strike, selling two calls (or puts) at a middle strike, and buying one call (or put) at a higher strike.

Objective: Profit from low volatility with minimal upfront cost.

Application: Suitable for investors expecting the underlying asset to remain close to the middle strike price. The maximum profit is achieved if the asset closes at the middle strike price at expiration. The risk is limited to the net premium paid.

g) Calendar Spread

Strategy: Involves selling a short-term option and buying a longer-term option with the same strike price.

Objective: Benefit from the differing rates of time decay.

Application: Suitable for investors who expect little movement in the underlying asset in the short term but a more significant move in the long term. The risk is limited to the net premium paid for the spread.

All these strategies provide a framework for achieving various investment objectives, from generating income to protecting against losses and speculating on market movements. Each strategy has its own risk-reward profile and suitability depending on the investor's market outlook, risk tolerance, and investment goals. Understanding these popular options strategies allows investors to tailor their approach to align with their specific financial objectives, which is exactly what I've done when designing the Slick strategy.

2. The Slick Trading Strategy

At this point, one might wonder why they should not choose one of the well-known and proven strategies. The truth is, when analysing them in detail with a practical approach, considering the skills and capital required as well as the expected reward, they all present issues that make them unsuitable for me, and probably for many other retail investors.

The covered call strategy requires buying at least 100 units of the selected stock. However, I lack the knowledge and expertise to determine which stock to buy. It doesn't do any good to gain a few dollars from selling a covered call option if your stock loses more than 30% of its initial value. Therefore, one needs to be able to pick the right stock to avoid the risk of losing value, which I am not able to do. Additionally, to generate a decent income from selling covered calls, one needs to own a significant number of stocks—a capital that I do not have and cannot invest.

The same situation applies to the wheel strategy, which may require even higher capital if the stock is assigned at a strike price significantly below the market level. In this case, selling call options might not generate meaningful income, and while being stuck with the purchased stock, additional capital would be needed to continue selling put options. And this is regardless of whether the assigned stock is one you are happy to own or not. If you want to continue generating regular income with the strategy, you will inevitably need more capital. That is the simple truth. Actually, I struggle to understand how such a flawed strategy can be so popular.

All other strategies work well when you are correct about the market's direction, which is not easy. I certainly do not possess the technical skills to determine that, and above all, I do not like the risk involved in being wrong. Strategies like the *iron condor, butterfly,* or *calendar spread* have a common drawback: if you lose, you may lose big, sometimes up to more than ten times what you would have made if you were right. This also applies to strategies like the *straddle* and *strangle* that do not require knowing the market direction.

The only way to manage this risk is by setting up a complex system of take profits and stop losses, which can be difficult to implement effectively, or by spending a considerable amount of time tracking market performance. Neither approach works for me, as I don't have the required technical expertise or the time to commit.

Ultimately, I do not favour any of these option strategies, and you shouldn't either if you value your hard-earned money. However, there is no need to worry. The *Slick strategy* addresses all these concerns. It requires minimal capital investment, limited market knowledge, and technical skills, as well as little time to implement, while still offering great returns.

2.1 General characteristics

The Slick Trading Strategy is designed to leverage specific market conditions and statistical insights. In this section, I will outline the general characteristics of the strategy, emphasizing its simplicity, low risk, and minimal capital requirements. I will explain how the strategy aims to capitalize on weekly movements of the S&P 500 index.

To ensure the robustness of this strategy, I conducted extensive backtesting over the last 10 years of S&P 500 data; I shared it with relatives and friends interested in trading, gathered their feedback, and saw that those who implemented it achieved remarkable results. I implemented it myself since the end of 2022, achieving significant profits while learning how to execute it effectively. These success stories, along with my own, serve as a testament to the strategy's potential and its applicability in real-world scenarios, even without professional trader qualifications.

Before delving into the details of the strategy, I must acknowledge that I am not a professional trader. My educational and professional background is rooted in law rather than in the economics and finance sectors typically associated with professional traders. I hold a University Degree in Law, a Specialization Certificate in Finance and Budgetary Law, and a Master's Degree in Contractual Law, and I have spent most of my professional career working in Procurement. I began investing in stocks in January 2018 and started trading options in 2020.

While I may not hold the title of a professional trader and have limited experience, my unique perspective has allowed me to explore the market without the constraints of conventional trading methodologies. This fresh approach led to the development of the strategy I am about to share with you in this book. However, **this isn't financial advice**. I'm simply sharing my personal journey to financial independence in the hope that you can learn from it. Please conduct your own studies, research, and verifications to make well-informed financial decisions adapted to your unique circumstances. Trading in financial markets involves risk, and it is essential to approach it with caution and a continuous learning mindset.

2.2 Key elements

At the beginning of 2022, I was searching for the right approach to option trading, but none of the main strategies appealed to me. *Covered calls* were prohibitively expensive, requiring the purchase of several packages of 100 stocks to generate a decent monthly income. I couldn't afford that approach, and besides, which stocks should I buy? Even excellent stocks like Google and Amazon were crashing in 2022. This was not what I was looking for.

I also heard a lot of enthusiastic traders online praising the *wheel strategy*, but when I dug deeper, I quickly realized it was much the same. Other popular strategies were too risky for my taste. However, everything changed when I discovered index options. I loved the idea of cash settlement—no need to choose or buy any security. This allowed me to implement various strategies without the hassle of selecting the right stock or investing large sums to buy or cover multiple packages of 100 stocks, which could cost thousands of dollars.

I began exploring some of the more popular strategies with index options, such as the famous *iron condor* and the *broken butterfly*. Despite their evocative names, neither met my expectations. Eventually, I stumbled upon a strategy called **the bull put spread**, which forms the base upon which I then developed the Slick strategy. Technically, the bull put spread is an options strategy typically used when a trader expects the price of the underlying asset—in this case, the S&P 500 Index (SPX)—to remain stable or experience a moderate rise.

However, instead of relying on market or technical analysis to predict whether the index will hold steady or increase, the Slick strategy adopts a different method. As you'll see in the following sections, this strategy is based on unique, personally developed, and backtested variations that depend solely on historical statistical market data and charts.

A *bull put spread* essentially involves being short a put option and long another put option with the same expiration but a lower strike price. In other words, it requires selling a put at a given strike price and simultaneously buying a put for protection at a lower strike price, both with the same expiration date. This way, the short put generates income, while the long put offsets assignment risk and protects the trader in case of a sharp downward move. To explain it better, let me give you an example, going back to August 19th, 2024, when the S&P 500 Index (SPX) was trading slightly above 5560. To implement a bull put spread, at that time, you could have:

1. **Sold a put option** with a strike price of 5560, expiring in one month on September 18th, 2024, for a premium of $1000 per option.
2. **Bought a put option** with a strike price of 5550, expiring on the same date (September 18th, 2024), for a premium of $690 per option.

In this scenario:

- The net *premium* received would have been $310 ($1000 received from the sold put minus $690 paid for the bought put).
- The maximum *profit* would have been the net premium received ($310 per option).
- The maximum loss, if the SPX falls below 5550, would be $690. This is calculated as the difference between the two strike prices

(10 index points multiplied by $100) minus the net premium received (in this case, $310).

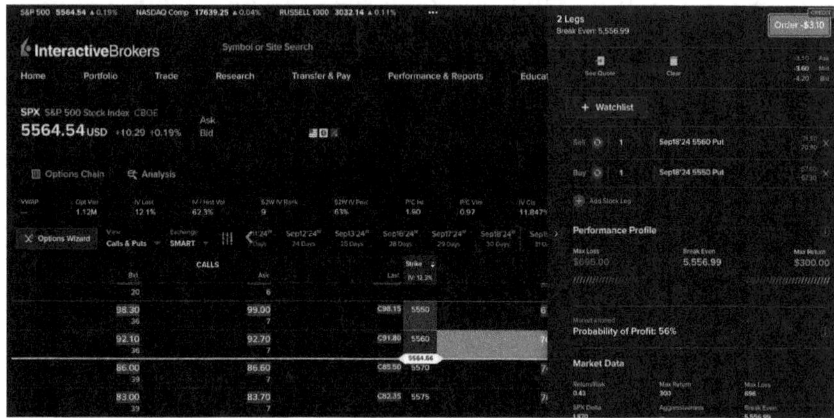

If the SPX stays above 5560, both options expire worthless, and you keep the premium as profit.

If the SPX falls below 5560 but stays above 5550, you may incur some losses, but they are limited by the long put at 5550.

If the SPX falls below 5550, your maximum loss is realized, but it's capped at $690 per option contract.

With this approach, based on historical data from the SPX index over the last 10 years, there is a slightly more than 75% (75.8%) chance of winning the trade. Statistically speaking, this means you can expect to win this trade on average 9 out of 12 months, resulting in the profitability detailed in the table below:

No of Option Contracts	Winning months	Losing months	Profits per month*	Total Profit	Losses per month	Total Loss	Annual Balance ($)
1	9	3	310	2,790	690	2,070	720

*Calculated pre-taxes based on recurring market prices for the same type of trade.

It may not seem like a lot of money at first, but if you repeat the trade ten times per month, selling 10 identical option contracts, the total annual income pre-taxes would be $12,000, as demonstrated in the table below. The capital investment would be $6,900, which is the maximum monthly loss. This approach would generate around 105% annual yield without reinvesting the proceeds. Not too bad, either!

No of Option Contracts	Winning months	Losing months	Profits per month*	Total Profit	Losses per month	Total Loss	Annual Balance ($)
10	9	3	3,100	27,900	6,900	20,700	7,200

*Calculated pre-taxes based on recurring market prices for the same type of trade.

However, the example illustrated above represents just the *standard way* to implement the *bull put spread*. It is important to remember that historical statistical data is not a guarantee of future performance but merely an indication. You should always have a *"margin of safety"* to address, inter alia, the statistical risk. In this example, losing the monthly trade just one or two more times than the statistical average could result in limited or no profit for the year and even lead to some losses. That is why the *Slick strategy* involves **unique variations** designed to **manage statistical risk** and **exponentially enhance overall profitability.**

2.3 The Slick Strategy's Unique Twists

The monthly *bull put spread*, as demonstrated above, looks promising but is still not exactly what I was looking for. The level of risk is still too high for my taste.

The strategy hinges on the historical growth trajectory of the S&P 500. Since its inception in March 1957, the index, designed to be a comprehensive, market-capitalization-weighted index representing the performance of 500 large companies listed on the U.S. stock exchange, has delivered an average annual return of approximately

10-11%, including reinvested dividends. This figure can vary depending on the exact period considered and the calculation method applied, but over the long term, this has been the widely accepted approximate average annual return.

According to the most acknowledged estimation, there has been, on average, a bearish market every 5.5 years since the creation of the S&P 500 index, with an average duration of 10 months. Therefore, on average, each decade consists of a bit more than 9 years in a bull market and a bit less than a year in a bear market. As a result, betting that the index will continue to grow month over month gives traders a hedge. But is such a hedge sufficient to achieve profitability? My short answer is *no*. Statistical data is a very useful tool, but as I have already mentioned, it is not a guarantee of future performance. A *margin of safety* is needed to manage the so-called *statistical risk*. In our context, statistical risk refers to the potential for a financial loss or an unfavourable outcome due to the inherent uncertainty in the statistical models or assumptions used to predict future events. In financial markets, statistical risk is often quantified using probabilities derived from historical data, and it can arise from various sources, such as market volatility, model inaccuracies, or unexpected events that weren't accounted for in the model. For example, in an investment strategy like the Slick one, statistical risk might involve the likelihood that returns will deviate from their expected values due to random fluctuations in the market. Understanding this concept is important for managing uncertainty and ensuring that there is a *margin of safety* to protect us against potential losses.

How can a margin of safety be incorporated into the strategy? To answer this question, a holistic approach that carefully considers all key aspects of the strategy must be applied.

Let me explain to you the **unique** aspects of the *Slick strategy.*

a) Expiration term

I first focused on the **expiration date**. It seemed somewhat intuitive to me that betting the index would close the month at a higher level than it was trading at the beginning of the month could be too risky due to several factors. A month is a long timeframe during which many events capable of significantly impacting the market can take place. The longer the period the trade is *"open,"* the higher the risk that the market direction changes against you. Additionally, betting on a monthly period limits the trades to only 12 per year. This means that a small variation from the statistical average data, say around 10%, can severely impact the profitability of the strategy. This would not apply if the trades were more numerous, such as when the strategy is implemented on a weekly or daily basis with 0DTE options. Finally, the premiums paid for monthly options are not significantly higher than those for shorter expiration date options. Therefore, using shorter-term options would likely not reduce profitability while potentially lowering risk.

Once I understood that, I had to decide which *shorter* timeframe would be most appropriate to effectively balance profitability and risk. It was not a complex task, but it required a lot of time to conduct all the relevant backtesting and calculations to identify the most suitable solution. Please note that I refer to it as *the most suitable solution,* because, in reality, there is no perfect solution; things may change depending on market conditions. However, based on my backtesting, the solution I identified proved to be the most effective in all market conditions.

I initially considered the daily timeframe, as the 0DTE index options seemed quite popular among traders. Trading daily offers the highest profitability since the trade is repeated about 250 times per year. During very strong bull markets, this trading frequency can be highly profitable. However, historical market data shows that, in the long term, the chances of success with this approach are just around 55%. Some traders use various techniques to determine when to implement the bull put spread. I've heard about complex indicators that, when combined, should be capable of signalling a bullish day with a certain degree of confidence. There are even online services based on algorithms or AI that can recommend whether it is going to be a good day to implement the strategy. However, as I mentioned from the beginning, my technical analysis skills are very basic, and I cannot rely on such online services due to their often prohibitive costs. Moreover, their declared rate of success (65% on average among the different services I found online) is not particularly impressive. Consequently, I discarded the 0DTE index options.

I then focused on the weekly expiration term. In this case, the historical data was much more encouraging, as I will show in detail in the next section on statistical data. With weekly expiration terms, the chances of winning the trade are slightly lower than with monthly terms (just over 72% vs. 75%). However, even with this difference, the weekly timeframe ensures significantly higher profitability, more than 120%, compared to the monthly timeframe, as demonstrated in the table below:

No of Trades	Winning months	Losing months	Profits per month*	Total Profit	Losses per month	Total Loss	Annual Balance ($)
12	9	3	310	2,790	690	2,070	720

No of Trades	Winning weeks	Losing weeks	Profits per week*	Total Profit	Losses per week	Total Loss	Annual Balance ($)
52	38	14	300	11,400	700	9,800	1,600

*Calculated pre-taxes based on the sale of **only one option** contract and recurring market prices for the same type of trade.

Even with weekly options, a trader can sell the same contract as many times as desired, depending on the capital allocated for this purpose.

If ten contracts are sold with a risk capital of $7,000, which would correspond to the maximum loss per week, the annual average profit based on historical data would be around $16,000, resulting in an annual yield of almost 230% without reinvesting the weekly profits. This also translates to approximately $1,300 average income per month.

I, therefore, concluded that shifting to a *weekly expiration cycle* could have significantly enhanced profitability and reduced risk compared to monthly cycles. This is attributed to shorter trade durations and increased trade frequency, allowing for better risk management. Even deviations of approximately 15% from average historical data, while potentially impacting profitability, are unlikely to result in meaningful losses.

Is it getting interesting? It will get even better!

b) Strike price

One of the first things that seemed strange to me when I first learned about the Bull Put Spread was the standard strike price. It felt illogical and somewhat risky to sell a put option at the same level as the market, as this implied betting on market growth. Naturally, I would have considered selecting a lower strike price for my put to reduce the risk of assignment.

My intuition was that selecting a strike price well out of the money would significantly increase my chances of a successful trade. However, it was essential to backtest this approach and, most importantly, evaluate its impact on the strategy's overall profitability.

After several tests and calculations using different strike prices, I eventually concluded that selling a put **30 points below** the market level at the opening of the first day of the trading week would significantly increase the strategy's success rate. On average, the success rate of the strategy would rise to just above **80%** as opposed to the **72%**

of the standard approach, while the profit would increase by almost **250%**, as indicated in the table below:

No of Trades	Winning weeks	Losing weeks	Profits per week*	Total Profit	Losses per week	Total Loss	Annual Balance ($)
52	42	10	300	12600	700	7000	5,600

*Calculated pre-taxes based on the sale of **only one option** contract and recurring market prices for the same type of trade.

This is quite unique! Typically, in the investment world, a lower risk level corresponds to a lower reward, meaning a lower profit. In this exceptional case, by selling the put contract out of the money, 30 points below the market level at the beginning of the trading week, a lower risk corresponds to a higher profit. This is because the significant reduction in the number of losing trades due to the implemented risk mitigation action greatly improves the cost profile, resulting in higher profit.

In 2023, for instance, this approach would have **reduced losses by almost 45%**. The total number of losing trades would have been 10 instead of 18, which would have resulted from applying the standard approach. This positively impacted the profitability of the strategy, which otherwise would not have yielded any profit that year.

c) Protection put level

The decision to opt for weekly terms posed a new issue. On the monthly timeframe, there is only the possibility to buy the protection put a minimum of 10 points below the one sold. Of course, one could always buy the protection put well below the minimum 10 points, increasing profits but also the relevant risk. This is an option that, due to my risk-averse nature, I almost immediately discarded. In contrast, the weekly terms offer the opportunity to buy the protection put a minimum of 5 points below the one sold. This may negatively impact the premium received, but it also dramatically reduces the risk. What would be the best solution? Instinctively, I would go for the less risky approach. However, emotions in investing often lead one down the wrong path. It is wiser to conduct thorough testing.

Most traders employing the *Bull Put Spread* strategy prefer to buy the protective put immediately after the one they have sold, typically just 5 points below. I assume the primary reason for this approach is to partially offset the risk of having sold an in-the-money put just above the market level. Others, more confident in their outlook, opt to buy the protective put at a much lower level, around 30-40 points below the sold put, to maximize profit potential.

None of such approaches seem to fit my specific situation. The Slick strategy does not involve selling an at-the-money put. As detailed in the previous, the approach is to sell a put approximately 30 points below the market level. Therefore, in principle, there is no need to buy the protective put just 5 points below, as there is no specific risk to offset. Additionally, I do not have any outlook on the market direction that would give me confidence in the trade's outcome. Therefore, I am unable to purchase the protective put significantly below the one I sell, which would increase my profits but also the associated risk.

The tests I conducted confirmed that buying the protective put only 5 points below the sold put significantly harms profitability, while buying the put 30-40 points below introduces excessive risk. The best solution lies somewhere in the middle: buying the protective put 10 points below the sold put, similar to the strategy typically employed in a monthly timeframe, despite executing this strategy on a weekly basis.

The following table shows all the different outcomes of the strategy depending on the level of the protective put purchased:

Level of the Protective put bought	No of Trades	Winning weeks	Losing weeks	Profit per week	Total Profit*	Losses per week	Total Loss	Annual Balance ($)
-5	52	42	10	120	5,040	380	3,800	1,240
-10	52	42	10	300	12,600	700	7,000	5,600
-20	52	42	10	610	25,620	1,390	13,900	11,720
-30	52	42	10	920	38,640	2,080	20,800	17,840

*Calculated pre-taxes based on the sale of **only one option** contract and recurring market prices for the same type of trade.

The table confirms that buying the protective put **ten points below** the one sold is the optimal solution. This strategy **increases profit by more than 350%** compared to the standard approach of buying the protective put just five points below the sold put, while the capital required for the trade — and therefore the associated risk — only increases by approximately **80%**. Clearly, the risk/reward ratio is much more favourable with this solution. Specifically, to gain $300 with this approach, one risks losing approximately 2.3 times that amount ($700). In contrast, with the standard approach, to achieve a profit of $120, the risk is losing 3.2 times that amount ($380).

While the alternatives at minus 20 and minus 30 points yield higher profits, the profit increase compared to the minus 10 option is relatively modest. Additionally, both options require significantly higher capital to execute the strategy and are, therefore, beyond my capacity and risk tolerance. As I mentioned from the beginning, I am risk-averse and do not aim to become a billionaire. My goal is to achieve a stable, regular income that can quickly lead to my financial independence, investing a limited amount of money. But of course, you need to make that decision based on your unique situation, risk appetite, and, ultimately, your objectives. I can only confirm that the strategy will work even with a protective put sold more than 10 points below the put you originally sold.

In any case, as detailed in the table below, the profit potential of the Slick strategy should not be underestimated. Instead of increasing the risk by widening the distance between the sold put and the protective put, it would be more appropriate to increase the number of option contracts sold per week. Using a weekly approach and purchasing a protective put 10 points below the sold put, based on historical SPX data from the last 10 years, the average annual profit from selling 10 option contracts would be $56,000, nearly $5,000 per month. This strategy requires a risk capital of just $7,000 per week and can generate **an impressive annual yield of 700%**. The table below shows different levels of profitability based on the number of option contracts sold. The column for potential losses per week also reflects the required risk capital.

No of Option Contracts sold	No of Trades	Winning weeks	Losing weeks	Profits per week*	Total Profit	Losses per week	Total Loss	Annual Balance ($)
5	52	42	10	1,500	63,000	3,500	35,000	28,000
10	52	42	10	3,000	126,000	7,000	70,000	56,000
15	52	42	10	4,500	189,000	10,500	105,000	84,000
20	52	42	10	6,000	252,000	14,000	140,000	112,000
25	52	42	10	7,500	315,000	17,500	175,000	140,000

*Calculated pre-taxes based on recurring market prices for the same type of trade.

It goes without saying that if such a profit is not sufficient for you, it is always possible to increase the number of option contracts sold per week beyond those indicated in the table above, thereby increasing the capital invested accordingly. Based on historical data, you could achieve very impressive gains, such as nearly $15,000 or $20,000 per month on average. I will explore this opportunity in detail later in the book, along with other techniques that can significantly enhance the overall strategy's profitability, while reducing the relevant risk.

d) Execution pauses

For the moment, you have all the main aspects of the Slick strategy:

A modified *bull put spread* executed weekly by selling a put contract on the SPX index at 30 points below its opening level at the beginning of the trading week, simultaneously combined with the purchase of a protective put with the same weekly expiration, but at least 10 points below the put sold.

However, at this point in my journey to develop the Slick strategy, one question still lingered: *Could I execute the strategy every week, irrespective of market conditions?*

The detailed analysis of historical data illustrated in the next section provided me with the answer to this key question. Specifically, historical data of the SPX showed that the strategy must be suspended when the 200-day moving average (200-DMA) moves above the level of the SPX. The 200-DMA is a technical analysis tool that calculates the average closing price of a security (in our case, the SPX) over the last 200 trading days.

This moving average is commonly used by investors and traders to assess the overall health and direction of a stock or market index. While this may sound like a complex technical analysis, I assure you it is not. With just a quick glance at the SPX chart, the status of the 200-DMA can be checked. I use a very basic chart provided online for free by *MarketWatch.com*, where the lines of the SPX and the 200-DMA are shown. The chart can be easily customized to allow the status of this indicator to be checked every week before initiating the trade.

As you can see in the picture below, the blue line represents the SPX, while the black line indicates the 200-DMA.

When the 200-DMA crosses above the SPX, it clearly signals negative market conditions, typically the start of a bearish market, under which the Slick strategy must **not** be executed.

Fortunately, this condition does not occur often in the market, as I will demonstrate in the next section. In other words, the weeks during which the strategy cannot be executed do not significantly impact its long-term profitability. By *"long term,"* I am not referring to a 10-year cycle, but rather the monthly average profit achievable through the strategy.

As an indicator, the 200-DMA mainly smooths out price fluctuations to help investors identify **long-term** trends. It is more effective at signalling the entrance of a bearish market than providing insights into short-term market movements.

There are two additional related indicators, the **10-DMA** and the **20-DMA,** that need to be considered for short-term purposes to determine whether the strategy can be executed in a given week. Both indicators are very similar to the 200-DMA and are also quite simple to analyse on the same chart.

Both moving average lines are short-term technical analysis indicators that calculate the average closing price of a security, in our case, the SPX, over the past 10 and 20 trading days, respectively. They help investors and traders identify short-term trends and potential entry or exit points in the market.

In the picture below, the black line indicates the 10-DMA, the blue line represents the SPX, and the red and green lines represent the 10-day and 20-day moving averages, respectively.

However, it must be understood that moving average indicators are considered lagging indicators because they are based on past price data. This means they reflect historical prices and thus react to market movements after they have occurred rather than predicting future price movements. For example, the 10-day moving average calculates the average closing price of a security over the past 10 days. If the price of the security increases steadily, the 10-day moving average will rise, but with a delay. Similarly, if the price drops, the moving average will also drop, but only after the price decline has been established. Because of this lag, moving averages are useful for confirming trends rather than forecasting them. This is especially true for moving average indicators designed to identify short-term movements like the 10-DMA and the 20-DMA.

So, *why do we need to consider them?*

These two indicators might come into play two or three times a year, especially during those so-called "*market corrections*" or "pullbacks." A market correction is generally defined as a decline of 10% or more from a recent peak. Even in a bullish year, it's not uncommon to see 1 to 2 such corrections. These corrections are part of normal market behaviour and can occur due to various factors, including economic data releases, geopolitical events, or changes in market sentiment. Apart from corrections, smaller pullbacks (declines of less than 10%) can also occur more frequently. These are typically seen as healthy for the market, providing opportunities for new buyers to enter at lower prices.

When analysing the historical data, particularly focusing on the weeks when the strategy would have been unsuccessful, a certain pattern became evident to me. Some losses were 'isolated.' This means that the week before the loss was successful, and the week after the loss, the trade was successful again. However, on average, half of the times when a loss occurred, another loss followed in the next week or the week after. When checking the corresponding historical charts, I realized that in such cases, a correction or pullback had taken place, and the 10-DMA and 20-DMA were both above the SPX level, as shown in the chart above, related to a pullback in August 2024.

With this in mind, I concluded that checking the chart, and in particular these two indicators, could have prevented continuing to execute the strategy when a correction or pullback had started. Of course, due to the nature of lagging indicators, it would not have been possible to avoid the first loss, but certainly, avoiding executing the strategy when both the 10-DMA and 20-DMA remained above the SPX line could have prevented additional losses in many instances.

Of course, this is not always exact. In some circumstances, this approach may lead to missed opportunities where the trade could have been perfectly successful. However, the analysis of historical data shows that this approach does not hinder the achievement of significant average profit over the entire period of strategy execution. On the contrary, the reduced number of losses incurred improves the strategy's overall profitability while reducing the statistical risk. When I backtested this approach, it turned out that the average number of **annual trade losses** during the analysed period (from 2014 to 2023) was **reduced to less than 5**, compared to **34 successful trades on average**. Consequently, **the strategy should have been paused for 13 weeks per year on average**, with an **overall success rate of around 87%.**

However, the number of *non-trading weeks* seemed to be heavily influenced by the data from 2022, a notably bearish year, during which the strategy remained inactive for an unprecedented 44 weeks. While it is necessary to account for any losses in 2022 to accurately assess the overall profitability of the strategy across the ten years analysed, including this year in the calculation of the average number of paused weeks per year may lead to misleading conclusions. After all, such a prolonged pause essentially amounts to a suspension of the strategy rather than a temporary halt. When we exclude the 44 weeks of inactivity in 2022, the analysis indicates that, on average, **the strategy would only be paused** for **9 weeks** per year, **with 38 successful trades** and still **only 5 resulting in losses**—reflecting a **success rate of over 88%.**

The table below summarizes the average outcome of this approach based on historical data and compares it with the standard one:

No of Traded weeks	Non trading weeks	Winning weeks	Losing weeks	Profits per week*	Total Profit	Losses per week	Total Loss	Annual Balance ($)
52	0	42	10	300	12,600	700	7,000	5,600
43	9	38	5	300	11,400	700	3,500	7,900

*Calculated pre-taxes based on the sale of **only one option** contract and recurring market prices for the same type of trade.

The data clearly confirms that considering the trends of the 10-DMA and 20-DMA has a significant impact on profitability. A comparison of the strategy's performance with and without these indicators reveals that **profit increases by over 40%** ($2,300). It is important to note that the positive impact on profit is not driven by an increase in premiums received. In fact, the total premiums received slightly decrease with this approach. The primary reason for the enhanced profitability lies in the significant **reduction in losses**, which decreases **by 50%**. As a result, when trading the Slick strategy, it's essential to recognize that while this approach enhances overall profitability, strict adherence to the pause criteria is vital, as this method is fundamentally designed to manage statistical risk.

In conclusion, the Slick strategy must not be executed when the 200-DMA is above the level of the SPX, no matter where the other two indicators are. In addition, it must not be executed when both the 10-DMA and the 20-DMA indicators are simultaneously above the SPX line, even if the 200-DMA is below the SPX. Of course, if the strategy is paused, it is then advisable to wait for the SPX line to cross back above **both DMA lines** before resuming the strategy."

Conversely, when only one of the Moving Average Lines, either the 10-DMA or the 20-DMA, is above the SPX, the strategy remains viable and should not be paused, as historical chart analysis indicates that this scenario seldom precedes a market downturn significant enough to cause a trade loss. There are only two exceptions. The first applies to the month of September, which historically is the worst month for stocks due to market seasonality. During this period, if at least one of the Moving Average lines, particularly the 10-DMA, is above the SPX line, the strategy should be paused and resumed only when the SPX rises back above both Moving Average lines. The second exception relates to national holidays, which affect the duration of the trading week. Usually, national holidays do not impact the implementation of the strategy when they fall on Tuesday, Wednesday, or Thursday, provided all the conditions to execute the strategy are fully met. However, during such weeks, if the 10-DMA is above the SPX, the strategy shall be paused. This is because, contrary to standard weeks, holiday periods can often affect market liquidity and volatility. In the presence of a negative signal, like the 10-DMA crossing above the SPX line, it could be too risky to execute the strategy. Additionally, when national holidays occur on Mondays or Fridays, since the premium received might be slightly lower due to the shorter duration of the trade, potentially increasing your financial risk for the week, the strategy must be paused not only when the 10-DMA is above the SPX line but also when, despite all moving averages being below the SPX line, an important economic event capable of significantly impacting market trends is scheduled during the last two days of the trading week, as there may not be sufficient time to recover if the market reacts unfavourably. In fact, in such a shortened week, a major economic event towards the end of the trading week could further increase unpredictability, making it again too risky to execute the strategy. The table below summarizes when the strategy can be executed or must be paused:

Condition	Strategy Execution	Strategy Paused
The 200-DMA is ABOVE the SPX line	NO	YES
The 200-DMA is BELOW the SPX line, and the 10-DMA and the 20-DMA are **both simultaneously ABOVE the SPX line**	NO	YES
The 200-DMA is BELOW the SPX, and either the 10-DMA or the 20-DMA is ABOVE the SPX in the month of September	NO	YES
The 200-DMA and the 20-DMA are both BELOW the SPX line, while the 10-DMA is ABOVE the SPX **in a shortened trading week due to national holidays**	NO	YES
The 200-DMA is BELOW the SPX line, and both the 10-DMA and the 20-DMA are simultaneously BELOW the SPX line in a shortened trading week due to national holidays occurring on Monday or Friday, with a major economic event scheduled in one of the last two days of the trading week	NO	YES
The 200-DMA is BELOW the SPX line, and both the 10-DMA and the 20-DMA are simultaneously BELOW the SPX line	YES	NO
The 200-DMA is BELOW the SPX, and either the 10-DMA or the 20-DMA is ABOVE the SPX line **in any month of the year, excluding September, and during a standard 5-day trading week**	YES	NO

Finally, as I mentioned earlier regarding the 200-DMA, analysing the 10-DMA and 20-DMA lines does not require any particular technical analysis skills. I believe that the claim that the strategy requires *little* market expertise is, therefore, confirmed. In relation to these indicators, one simply needs to access a pre-set chart showing the three lines and check their positions with regard to the SPX line.

In the step-by-step video guide, I will demonstrate, using the free charting available on *MarketWatch.com*, how to quickly and easily set up the chart for all three indicators.

2.4 Historical Market Data Analysis

By now, it must be pretty clear to you that the Slick strategy leans heavily on statistics. I've often said, *"based on historical data... you can do this and that…"*. But how reliable is this? Can we really expect that things will unfold in the future the same way they did in the past?

In this section, I will provide a detailed explanation of the statistical data that supports my thesis on the strategy's profitability. Specifically, I will present the statistical foundation of the Slick strategy based on the past 10 years of SPX data. My aim is to demonstrate how the S&P 500 index typically behaves, focusing on the probability of weekly gains and minimal losses.

While such an analysis may involve a lot of *boring* numbers, I am confident this mathematical approach will accurately illustrate to you the historical performance of the SPX, fully demonstrating the Slick strategy's reliability and potential profitability within a reasonable *margin of safety.*

As I mentioned earlier, when developing the strategy, I first analysed the SPX's growth trend since its establishment in March 1957. Once I was sufficiently confident that betting on the continuous growth of the index year after year provided traders with a hedge, I downloaded the SPX historical data from MarketWatch.com, covering the period from 2004 to the end of 2013 — 10 years in total — To assess the effectiveness of this hedge over the entire period, as well as on a year-by-year and week-by-week basis.

For the geeks who want to dive deeper into the numbers, the detailed analysis year by year and week by week is provided at the end of this book, together with the AI verification on the backtesting analysis conducted.

Below, I am presenting a summary table that shows the performance of the Slick strategy over the past 10 years, assuming a **weekly investment of $7,000, selling ten option contracts per week**. I excluded from the analysis the weeks when the 200-DMA alone, or both the 10-DMA and 20-DMA together, were above the SPX level, and thus the strategy could not be executed.

Year	Trading Week	Non-trading Weeks	Trades won	Trades Lost	Total Premium***	Total Losses	Annual Balance
2023	52	13	33	6	99,000	42,000	57,000
2022	52	0	5	3	15,000	21,000	-6,000
2021	52	5	39	8	117,000	56,000	61,000
2020	53	13	32*	7	93,080	49,000	44,080
2019	52	6	42	4	126,000	28,000	98,000
2018	52	23	27	2	81,000	14,000	67,000
2017	52	-	50	2**	150,000	5,240	144,760
2016	52	7	41	4	123,000	28,000	95,000
2015	53	13	34	6**	102,000	4,170	97,830
2014	53	6	41*	6**	122,200	40,570	81,630
Annual Average					102,828	28,798	74,030
Grand total					1,028,280	287,980	740,300
Monthly Average Income							6,169

*Two trades only partially successful.
**One trade only partially unsuccessful.
***Calculated pre-taxes, based on recurring market prices for the same type of trade.

The analysis indicates that the strategy would have been extremely profitable, yielding an average profit of almost 1,000% annually for a total income of **$740,300** over the entire period analysed, excluding the powerful compound effect of reinvesting the proceeds. This profit corresponds, on average, to an annual income of **$74,030,** which translates into a monthly average income of **$6,169**, including the weeks and months during which the strategy should not have been executed.

This would have been an outstanding performance, especially considering that during the period in question, there were three bear markets, which is quite an exceptionally high number. And do not forget that the calculation is based on **ten option contracts sold** weekly, for which the required risk capital is just **$7,000**; as promised, a very small capital investment.

It is also worth noting that during the three bear markets, excluding 2022, which was predominantly bearish and caused the interruption of the strategy implementation, the other bearish periods in 2018 and 2020 still allowed the Slick strategy to deliver excellent returns. In my view, this is a remarkable testament to the strategy's ability to effectively manage the risks associated with deviations from statistical data.

Of course, it must be mentioned that in the market data analysis above, the amount of the premiums received and paid is calculated based on today's values, not those applicable during past years. However, this does not affect the overall profitability and consistency of the strategy, as these are maintained primarily by its structure and the particular nature of the index option.

First of all, it must be acknowledged that using today's market values to calculate the premiums for 2021, 2022, and 2023 is somewhat reasonable because the market conditions are likely similar enough for these recent years. But above all, as I said, it is the nature of the index options and the structure of the strategy that provides a significant degree of consistency. Indeed, the strategy involves selling a put option and buying a protective put 10 points below. The net premium (the difference between the sold put and the protective put) is what matters. Since the amount at stake is consistently $100 per point (i.e., $1,000 in total), the income generated by the strategy is more a function of this structure rather than the absolute value of the index. Therefore, while the exact premium values from previous years might introduce minor variations, the income from the strategy should be relatively consistent because the risk and reward are based on the same $1,000 per 10-point difference, regardless of the underlying index value.

Other aspects to be considered are that historical volatility and specific market conditions can affect premiums. Changes in option premiums may result from market sentiment, interest rates, and other factors. Higher volatility generally increases option premiums, potentially increasing profits from selling puts. However, it also increases the cost of protective puts, providing some sort of consistent balancing.

I must also mention that all my calculations do not account for the commission fees charged by your broker, the taxes you will need to pay on the proceeds, or any possible currency conversion costs in

US dollars. Therefore, whenever I refer to *income*, I mean *operational income*, and when I refer to *profit*, I mean *gross profit*.

This is because commission fees vary significantly between brokers; some may offer commission-free trading while compensating with higher spreads between the buy and sell prices. Additionally, fiscal systems differ widely across the globe, making it impossible to estimate applicable taxes, which are closely tied to your personal financial situation. The same applies to currency conversion costs, which cannot be calculated generically. Nonetheless, considering the significant profit margin provided by the Slick strategy, these additional costs do not undermine the overall positive assessment of the strategy's profitability.

Finally, even though the past market data analysis is quite extensive and shows that the strategy would have been very profitable, suggesting potential for future profitability, it is crucial to understand that there is no guarantee it will work the same way in the coming years. However, I have personally executed the strategy since the end of 2022 up to the present day, and my data confirms its extremely high profitability. This hands-on experience has also provided me with invaluable insights into executing the strategy, which I will explain in the following chapters. Properly applying these techniques could significantly reduce statistical risk and, more generally, improve overall risk management and, thus, the profitability of the strategy.

2.5 Statistical Data Risk Assessment

In my preamble, I claim that the Slick strategy involves **little** risk. All in all, I believe that the historical market data analysis I shared with you confirms that the Slick strategy, as promised, can deliver extremely good returns with little capital requirement and, consequently, based on its historical performance, it also entails very *little* risk.

The table below, based on the historical market data, shows what could be, **on average,** the returns of the Slick strategy depending on the number of option contracts sold each week:

No of Option Contracts sold	No of Trades	Winning weeks	Losing weeks	Profits per week*	Total Profit	Losses per week	Total Loss	Annual Balance ($)
5	43	38	5	1,500	57,000	3,500	17,500	39,500
10	43	38	5	3,000	114,000	7,000	35,000	79,000
15	43	38	5	4,500	171,000	10,500	52,500	118,500
20	43	38	5	6,000	228,000	14,000	70,000	158,000
25	43	38	5	7,500	285,000	17,500	87,500	197,500

*Calculated pre-taxes based on recurring market prices for the same type of trade considering 10 option contracts sold.

However, as noted before, historical market data, no matter how extensive or robust, cannot guarantee future performance.

While the table above represents the average performance of the strategy, the table below illustrates the strategy's performance if the worst data from the past decade were used in the calculation. Specifically, the highest number of lost trades occurred in 2021, with 8 losses, and the year with the fewest winning trades was 2018, with only 27 successful trades.

In the unlikely event that we encounter such unfavourable circumstances in a very unlucky year, the strategy would still remain profitable. In fact, given such data and assuming the strategy was paused for 17 weeks, the strategy's performance, depending on the number of option contracts sold, would look as follows:

No of Option Contracts sold	No of Non-Trading weeks	Winning weeks	Losing weeks	Profits per week*	Total Profit	Losses per week	Total Loss	Annual Balance ($)
5	17	27	8	1,500	40,500	3,500	28,000	12,500
10	17	27	8	3,000	81,000	7,000	56,000	25,000
15	17	27	8	4,500	121,500	10,500	84,000	37,500
20	17	27	8	6,000	162,000	14,000	112,000	50,000
25	17	27	8	7,500	202,500	16,750	134,000	68,500

*Calculated pre-taxes based on recurring market prices for the same type of trade

If this were your worst trading year, it would still appear very profitable, wouldn't it?

To further validate the limited risk associated with implementing the Slick strategy, the table below analyses the number of unsuccessful trades needed to incur a loss, based on the strategy's average historical performance and assuming a consistent number of non-trading weeks.

Trading Week	No of Option contracts	Non-trading Weeks	Trades won	Trades Lost	Total Premium*	Total Losses	Annual Balance
52	10	9	38	5	114,000	35,000	79,000
52	10	9	37	6	111,000	42,000	69,000
52	10	9	36	7	108,000	49,000	59,000
52	10	9	35	8	105,000	56,000	49,000
52	10	9	34	9	102,000	63,000	39,000
52	10	9	33	10	99,000	70,000	29,000
52	10	9	32	11	96,000	77,000	19,000
52	10	9	31	12	93,000	84,000	9,000
52	10	9	30	13	90,000	91,000	- 1,000

*Calculated based on recurring market prices for the same type of trade.

The analysis indicates that a deviation of **160%** (accounting for 8 additional unsuccessful trades per year) from the average market historical performance over the last 10 years would be required to produce a minor loss. While this scenario is not impossible, it is highly unlikely. Even when we disaggregate the historical data year by year, focusing on each individual year's performance rather than the average, we find that not a single year in the past decade has come close to such a significant deviation. The highest number of lost trades occurred in 2021, with 8 losses, still far from the 13 unsuccessful trades needed to incur a loss.

Using a similar approach, the table below analyzes the number of unsuccessful trades needed to incur a loss, based on the worst historical performance of the Slick strategy. The table shows that the data would need to worsen by approximately 40% before any minor losses would occur.

Winning weeks	Losing weeks	Profits per week*	Total Profit	Losses per week	Total Loss	Annual Balance ($)
27	8	300	8100	700	5600	2500
26	9	300	7800	700	6300	1500
25	10	300	7500	700	7000	500
24	11	300	7200	700	7700	-500

*Calculated on the basis of only one option contract sold and recurring market prices for the same type of trade.

Market gurus often assert that the infamous belief that *"this time is different"* is flawed, as history tends to repeat itself. I am not suggesting that this time is different; rather, I am relying on the expectation that it will be much the same.

Furthermore, even in the unlikely event that such a dramatic deviation from the historical performance of the SPX should occur in a given year, it is highly improbable that it would also happen either in the preceding year or the following one. Therefore, if the strategy is consistently implemented, the proceeds from just one of those years would be sufficient to offset such a minor loss. The 2022 data presented in the previous section confirms this, even though the minor loss recorded ($3,600) was not due to a deviation from historical market data, but rather to the interruption of the strategy execution at the start of a bearish period.

Ultimately, after thorough consideration, I firmly believe that the Slick strategy goes beyond being a simple bull put spread. It integrates a set of unique features that enable effective statistical risk management without compromising the simplicity of its execution, which I will detail in the next chapter.

3. Implementation Modalities

In this section, I will outline the exact procedure for implementing the Slick strategy, which I developed through both backtesting and real-time testing. These steps are as important as the strategy structure itself. Execution mistakes can completely undermine the strategy's profitability, no matter how good the strategy is.

Once you have fully understood the structure and main aspects of the Slick strategy, there are still many elements related to its implementation that need to be addressed. I'm sure that many questions are lingering in your mind right now.

When should I enter the trade? Should I place an order before the market opens, or wait for the opening? If I wait, when exactly should I place my order—immediately after the opening, or should I wait a bit? If waiting, how long should I wait? How frequently should I monitor the trade? Should I monitor it at all? And if the trade turns against me, are there any corrective measures I should undertake?

You will find clear answers to all these questions and more in the following sections. These recommended procedures for the implementation of the strategy are the result of in-depth data and chart analysis, followed by years of direct practice. The most important lesson I have learned, which I believe is essential to convey to you, is that if you do not follow these procedures, you may be lucky for a while, but don't be fooled; in the long term, the strategy will not work and won't yield the expected outcome. So, please read these sections carefully. Even if you may not agree with everything recommended here, give it a try. You will not be disappointed!

3.1 How to initiate the trading strategy

This is perhaps the most important section of the entire book. The activities illustrated here are at the heart of executing the strategy. Once you fully understand and practice them, you will master the Slick strategy.

The Slick strategy involves selling a put on the SPX 30 points below the opening price at the beginning of the trading week, with an expiration date at the end of the same trading week, while simultaneously buying a put 10 points below the one sold with exactly the same expiration date. As illustrated in the step-by-step video guide, when I say the selling and purchasing of the puts must be conducted simultaneously, I mean within *the same transaction*, not as separate operations. I also refer to the *"trading week"* instead of specific days like Monday and Friday because national holidays can cause the trading week to start or end on different days.

Having said that, there are three pressing questions when implementing the Slick strategy for the first time:

1. *Is there a specific period of the year to start it?*
2. *How many option contracts should one sell?*
3. *How and when should the order to initiate the trade be placed?*

Let's dig into it!

Is there a specific period of the year to start it?

You can start the strategy at any time, as long as it is the first trading day of the week and both the 10-DMA and 20-DMA are simultaneously below the SPX line, along with the 200-DMA. However, the best time to start the strategy is after a pullback or a market correction. This occurs when the SPX line crosses back above the 10-DMA and 20-DMA following a previous downturn.

In this case, it is better to wait one more week after the crossing to consolidate the uptrend before starting to trade the strategy. This approach gives you a much greater chance of beginning the implementation with a streak of four to five winning weeks, which would help build a buffer to handle any future downturns. Additionally, for the same reasons, it is advisable to follow this approach when you wish to increase the number of option contracts sold each week.

In general, I strongly recommend paper trading the strategy for a month or two before implementing it with real money. It is crucial to get familiar with the relevant procedures to avoid possible execution errors.

How many option contracts should one sell?

To answer this question, one criterion you certainly need to consider should be your investment capacity. In this regard, you must be aware that your broker may require a minimum deposit in your account to allow you to trade options. This amount may vary depending on your country of residence.

Additionally, for each option contract you sell, your broker requires sufficient funds in your account to fully cover your potential losses. This amount is usually calculated as the difference between the strike prices of the two put options (the one sold, and the one purchased) minus the premium received. In the case of the Slick strategy, this will be around $700 per option contract sold ($1,000 - $300 = $700).

However, some brokers may require you to deposit the full amount derived from the difference between the strike prices of the two put options, which would be $1,000 per option contract sold, disregarding the premium received.

The table below provides the estimated amounts required depending on the number of option contracts you may wish to sell. Please note that the capital at risk is calculated considering the estimated premiums receivable.

No of Option Contracts Sold	Capital Required ($)	Capital at Risk ($)
1	1,000	700
5	5,000	3,500
10	10,000	7,000
15	15,000	10,500
20	20,000	14,000
25	25,000	17,500

Based on the most common broker rules and recurring market prices for the same trade.

When considering the capital at risk in the Slick strategy, it's important to understand that the indicated amount is per week. However, this does not mean that you need to multiply this amount by 52 to cover the entire trading year and make that sum available in your broker account. The weekly figure represents the maximum potential loss in a single week. Historical data shows that experiencing two consecutive losses is extremely unlikely. In fact, based on historical market data, there has never been a case of two trades lost in the same month. You are more likely to experience a streak of successful trades, which further emphasizes that there's no need for additional capital beyond what is required on a weekly basis.

To simplify things and avoid the need to deposit additional funds throughout the year, I recommend depositing three times the minimum weekly amount when you begin trading the Slick strategy. This approach provides a more than sufficient buffer, ensuring that you are well-covered for any potential fluctuations over the course of the year.

In any case, your financial capacity should only be a secondary criterion when deciding how many option contracts to sell. The most important, and I would say the critical factor, is what you are emotionally capable of handling. The amount indicated under the column 'Capital at Risk' represents the losses you may and will experience from time to time. While data shows that the long-term implementation of this strategy typically leads to full recovery of such losses, you must be prepared to endure these setbacks when they occur. Otherwise, you may make poor decisions that could hinder your ability to successfully implement the strategy. More on this can be found in the chapter dedicated to managing your emotions.

Regardless of your decision, it is essential to understand that once you make a choice, you should better stick to it for 52 consecutive weeks, calculated including those weeks during which the strategy is paused (i.e., when the 200-DMA is above the SPX line, or the 10-DMA and 20-DMA are both simultaneously above the SPX line). At least you should avoid reducing the number of option contracts sold.

This consistency is preferable because changing, and in particular reducing, the number of option contracts sold during the 52-week cycle can harm the profitability of the strategy. Unsuccessful trades are not evenly distributed throughout the cycle; they are likely concentrated in specific periods due to market corrections and pullbacks. If you execute the strategy of selling ten option contracts during such a period, your losses will reflect this. Conversely, if you later reduce the number of option contracts sold, your income will decrease accordingly, negatively affecting the balance of gains and losses throughout the strategy cycle.

The table below illustrates a possible scenario where you initially start the strategy by selling 10 option contracts, but after incurring some losses, you decide to take a more cautious approach and switch to selling only 5 option contracts. The results are compared with those of sticking to your initial choice:

No of Option contracts sold	No of Trades executed	Winning trades	Losing Trades	Total Profit*	Total Loss	Balance of the first part of the 52-week cycle in ($)
10	10	6	4	18,000	28,000	-10,000

No of Option Contracts sold	No of Trades executed	Winning Trades	Losing Trades	Total Profit*	Total Loss	Balance of the second part of the 52-week cycle ($)
5	28	27	1	42,000	3,500	38,500
					Balance of the entire cycle	28,500

No of Option contracts sold	No of Trades executed	Winning trades	Losing Trades	Total Profit*	Total Loss	Balance of the entire cycle ($)
10	38	33	5	114,000	35,000	79,000

*Calculated pre-taxes based on recurring market prices for the same type of trade, and assuming that the strategy is not executed during 9 weeks with 5 lost trades in total, in line with the average resulting from historical market data backtesting.

The negative impact on the strategy's profitability is quite evident. It results in a loss of profit of roughly more than **60%**.

While it is ideal to thoughtfully determine the number of option contracts to sell over a 52-week period and remain consistent with that decision, a more conservative approach of starting with a smaller investment and gradually increasing it can also be viable as long as it is part of a comprehensive plan that you can strictly follow. Sticking to your trading plan is critical. When I was paper trading the strategy, I realized that starting with a smaller investment—by selling a limited number of option contracts—makes sense. It allows you to become familiar with the execution process and avoid mistakes before scaling up your investment. However, I also found that after a losing trade, there is often a temptation to increase your investment by selling more option contracts in an attempt to recover losses, driven by the incorrect assumption that another loss is less likely after one. Conversely, after a series of successful trades, you might be tempted to prematurely increase the number of contracts sold before following the guidelines outlined in your well-thought-out plan. This could lead to unexpectedly higher losses, which may significantly impact your previous gains.

That's why it's essential to develop a trading plan that clearly establishes how long you will trade a specific number of option contracts and when you will increase them. Without such a plan, the risk of making *emotionally-driven* decisions increases, potentially harming the strategy's overall performance—a topic we will explore further in the book.

How and when should the order to initiate the trade be placed?

The third question is how and when to place the order to initiate trading the strategy. There are several options, with the most common ones being as follows:

- Place an order before the market opens, 30 points below the closing level of the last day of the previous trading week, at the market price.

- Place an order immediately, within the first 5 minutes of the market opening, at the desired price.
- Place an order within the first 15 minutes following the market opening, at the desired price.
- Place an order later during the day but before the close of the first day of the trading week, at the desired price.

Placing an order before the market opens is absolutely a **NO**. This option carries significant risk because the market can open at a substantially different level than it closed, leading to an order execution that does not meet the desired criteria in terms of distance (minus 30 points) from the market opening level.

Place an order immediately at the market opening to ensure that your order is executed close to the opening level, minimizing the risk of significant index movements that can occur shortly after the market opens. However, this approach carries the risk of not achieving the desired price, as executing the order immediately would require placing it at the market price, which could be lower than the desired price. Therefore, my recommendation is to attempt executing the order at the desired price, rather than the market price, within the first 5 minutes after the opening.

Placing an order within the first 15-30 minutes following the market opening allows for some initial market volatility to settle, potentially providing a more stable price for execution. However, there is still a risk of rapid price changes during this period. Therefore, **I recommend this option only when there is concrete evidence that the market will open at a substantially lower level than it closed the previous week.** In this case, the initial minutes following the opening present a concrete opportunity to take advantage of downward market movement, which may allow selling the put at a much lower level than if the order had been placed immediately after the opening. The same could apply if the evidence showed the possibility for the market to open at a **substantially higher level** than it closed the previous week. In such a situation, entering immediately may result in a higher entry point than the market opening. Instead of chasing the market in an upward move, it is advisable to wait for the first 10-15 minutes after the opening, when volatility may settle a bit, allowing for a potential small retracement of the SPX before making an entry, which could typically be at a level closer to the actual opening of the index.

Substantial market movements may be driven by economic data released before the market opens. For this reason, it is advisable to check both the market calendar and the SPX futures trends before the market opens, so you can be prepared for the upcoming market activity.

Placing an order later during the day but before the close of the first day of the trading week provides the flexibility to observe market movements and choose a more optimal entry point. However, it requires constant monitoring and may miss the initial momentum of the market open. Overall, I believe this approach carries too much risk, as you may not be able to initiate the trade at the desired level (30 points below the SPX opening value). Additionally, it requires significant effort to monitor the market for several hours, which contradicts the principles governing the Slick strategy (specifically, little effort). Therefore, it does not meet my requirements.

This option would only be acceptable if, for any reason beyond your control, you have not been able to initiate the trade earlier in the day. In this case, if possible, the trade should be initiated between 12:00 pm and 1:30 pm (ET). Lunchtime is often considered a good moment to start a trade because the initial market volatility has settled, and traders have had time to digest and react to the morning's news and data releases. This typically results in a more stable and predictable trading environment.

However, if you have any doubts, as a general recommendation, executing the trade immediately after the market opens should be the preferred option. At the end of the day, it's essential to remember that what matters most is ensuring the trade is executed as close as possible to the SPX opening level.

Regardless of the approach you follow to initiate trading, your main objective should be to obtain a total premium in the range of $270-$330, which is deemed acceptable. However, in some circumstances, due to market conditions, it may not be possible to stay within this range. If the premium received is slightly lower than the range, it is better to accept it anyway rather than reducing the number of points of the put to be sold to only 25 or even 20 below the market level. This approach would excessively increase the risk. It is better to cash in a lower premium instead of losing the trade. Ultimately, it would not significantly impact the performance of the strategy as an unsuccessful trade would. On the contrary, if the premium offered when opening the trade appears to be higher than the range, there are two different possibilities, the first one being quite common and the second one fairly rare:

- If the premium is just slightly higher, by some $10-$20, you should simply cash it in and thank the market volatility for it.
- If the premium is significantly higher than the normal range, more than $40-$50, it probably means that the market is expecting a change in trend and a possible pullback. In such cases, you should increase the number of points below the market level for the sale of your put until you can obtain a premium within the expected range to reduce your risk as much as possible. However, if the market calendar indicates the release of critical economic data, which could be the reason for the negative outlook, or there are other geopolitical events scheduled for the week, that can significantly impact the market trend, you should

consider pausing the strategy for that week. Such a decision would not significantly impact the profitability of the strategy, since situations like this are not frequent.

Finally, if market conditions allow for an early close of the trade before its expiration date (more on that in the dedicated section), and you decide to proceed accordingly, do not start a new trade until the first day of the following trading week. Otherwise, you would unnecessarily increase the risk. Do not forget that the historical market data on which the strategy is based considers the probability of the SPX closing at a level not below 30 points from its opening level at the beginning of the trading week, not the level in the middle of the previous week. In other words, by opening a new trade earlier, you would not be aligned with the statistical data that supports the strategy. Hence, you would be taking an unnecessary risk. This also applies when the strategy has been paused because the 200-DMA, or both the 10-DMA and the 20-DMA, have crossed above the SPX line. Under these circumstances, the chart will eventually show a situation that allows for executing the strategy again. It is also likely that this will occur during the trading week. However, for the same reasons mentioned above regarding early trade close, the strategy execution should only resume on the first day of the following trading week.

To help you establish best practices, I have listed the activities to initiate the trade in the correct sequence below. All these activities together should not require more than 30-45 minutes of your time. Besides some very basic monitoring activities, which would not engage you for more than 30 minutes during the trading week, this is all you would need to do on a weekly basis. I believe this meets my claim of requiring *little* time to execute, as I mentioned in my preamble.

You can also review these actions in the step-by-step video guide included as a bonus with this book:

1. On the first day of the trading week, typically Monday morning before the market opens (or the day before, usually Sunday), check the charts to ensure that the 200-DMA and both the 10-DMA and the 20-DMA are below the SPX line, confirming that the strategy can be implemented.

2. At the same time, check the Market Calendar for the week. Specifically, look for any economic data releases on the first trading day that could significantly impact the market. This is crucial because favourable data may cause the index to open higher, while unfavourable data might lead to a lower opening. In such cases, it's advisable to wait a few minutes after the opening for volatility to settle before initiating the trade. However, if the market responds positively to the data, an immediate entry may also be a good option.

3. To confirm the expected market direction, it is important to check the SPX futures (E-Mini S&P 500 Future Continuous Contract) a few minutes before the opening, especially if the trend appears negative. In such a case, it might be wiser to wait a few minutes after the opening before initiating the trade. This allows you to sell the put at a lower level than the market opening if the downtrend continues.

4. At the opening, based on all the information and data collected, initiate the trade according to the modalities previously indicated in this chapter.

5. Once the order has been executed, verify that everything is in order and there have been no mistakes. It is not uncommon for transactions to be set incorrectly, such as inverting the put to be sold with the one to be bought. Spotting such mistakes immediately allows for effective remedies.

6. In case an operational error resulting from unintentional actions

or failures is detected, it should be immediately corrected. The most common errors include the inversion between the put to be sold and the one to be purchased, or mistakes related to the expiration date, which may be incorrect for at least one of the puts involved in the trade. Whether the trade can then be initiated with the correct procedure greatly depends on when the operational error has been detected. Usually, this remedy is applicable on the first day of the trading week. However, during the week, it is advisable to refrain from trade execution and wait for the next trading week.

Ultimately, this is all part of *the art of investing*. You will improve in managing this step in the strategy with practice. Personally, without any prior guidance, it took me a couple of months to get comfortable with these steps. However, with the help of this book, I am confident you can learn how to initiate the trade much faster.

3.2 How to monitor the trade

Once you have initiated the trade, do you need to monitor it? If so, how and how often?

Let me start by clearly stating that monitoring the trade is not particularly necessary. However, if you enjoy it and have the time, go for it. Regularly monitoring the index can give you a better sense of market trends over time. You may become familiar with certain directional movements, and this can help when initiating the trade for the strategy implementation.

Ultimately, monitoring the trade is about managing your emotions. If you can't manage your emotions to avoid critical execution mistakes, it's better to forget about the ongoing trade and wait until the market closes on the last day of the trading week to check the outcome.

So, when could monitoring the trade be helpful?

The truth is, there is only one circumstance where monitoring can be helpful. This is when the market rises rapidly in the first two days of the trading week, allowing you to close the trade by paying a small amount, typically between **$20 to $30 per trade**. Normally, you do not need to close the trade early. However, if the *market calendar* indicates the release of critical economic data in the last two days of the trading week, which could significantly impact market trends, it is advisable to close the trade to avoid unnecessary risk.

I personally like monitoring my trade, but I am not obsessed with it. I try not to get emotional and limit the time I dedicate to the strategy. I mainly monitor my trade once or twice a day for a few minutes, especially towards market closing. I keep a closer eye on the strategy if the trade is moving rapidly in my favour. In this case, I assess the possibility of closing it early based on the market calendar and the current geopolitical situation. I know this approach might be challenging for some, as deciding whether and when to close a trade can be tough. Remember, the strategy works well even if you don't act. Like with trade initiation, practice will help you get better at managing this part of the process.

At the end of the trading week, typically on Fridays, I may also choose to close my trade early if market conditions permit. In such cases, I reduce the cost cap to $10-$15 per contract. However, this approach is not mandatory, as the strategy performs effectively either way. I prefer this method to avoid unnecessary risks when a trade can be closed at a reasonable cost.

It's important to note that consistently closing trades early, when feasible, has minimal to no impact on the strategy's estimated profitability, previously presented. While there is a cost associated with the early close of trades, which reduces the premium received from the option contracts sold at the start of the trading week, the statistical data does not account for the possible savings generated by reduced losses from this risk mitigation measure. In fact, if just one trade is saved by this approach every two years, it would compensate for all the costs incurred up to that point. It must be remembered that, although unlikely, there is always a possibility that a given situation, sometimes unexpected, could turn a successful trade into a losing one.

3.3. How to close the trade

At the end of the trading week, when the trade reaches its expiration date, an out-of-the-money option will expire worthless, making the premium received at the start of the week your profit. Conversely, if the option expires in-the-money, it will be automatically exercised or settled for its intrinsic value by your broker, meaning you will be charged $1,000 per option contract sold. This amount, minus the premium received, constitutes your total loss. Regardless of the outcome, no action is required from your side.

As mentioned in the previous section, you may want to close the trade early before expiration by paying a small amount to lock in profits. In such cases, you need to take action. The exact steps vary from one broker to another. However, it is critical that the close is done in a single simultaneous transaction, not in separate operations to buy back the sold put and sell the protective put previously purchased.

Most major brokers offer the capability to set up these types of orders. I use Interactive Brokers, a reputable American broker that is also widely used in Europe and Asia. In the step-by-step video guide, I'll demonstrate how to close a trade before expiration using Interactive Brokers. Of course, it goes without saying that you can use any other broker you trust.

3.4 Corrective actions

One of the most frequently asked questions when I started sharing the Slick strategy with relatives and friends was whether any corrective actions could be implemented if the trade turned against us. The short and honest answer to this question is that, for all practical purposes, there are no corrective actions that can be effectively implemented to save the trade.

Some traders may set up complex mechanisms of take profits and stop losses. However, this is easier said than done. In a strategy like the Slick one, involving index options, this approach may result in overall lower profits. This is because stop-loss orders can be triggered prematurely, even when the market direction might have reversed by the end of the trading week, resulting in a successful trade. To limit this risk, stop-loss orders should be set up in a way that, due to the particular nature of the index option, they would allow only minor cost savings, likely below 20% of the total amount, meaning some $100 out of a total $700 estimated loss per trade. Additionally, since the market direction can always reverse before the end of the trading week, one might risk losing $600 to save $100. Market reversals are not just theoretical; they happen in practice. During my trial-and-error phase, it happened to me twice in less than a year. This experience was enough to show me that trying to save a small amount by setting up complex mechanisms isn't worth the effort.

In reality, traders who use this method usually do not buy the protective put or buy it at a much lower level. In such cases, setting up a mechanism for stop losses can be appropriate. However, I do not prefer this approach, as profits can still be negatively affected by unnecessary stop losses triggered too early. Additionally, losses can be higher than anticipated due to overnight risk. This risk refers to the potential for significant market movements that occur when markets are closed, which can impact the effectiveness of stop-loss orders. In other words, when the market opens the next day, the price might have moved significantly from the previous day's closing price, causing a gap. If the price gap is past the stop-loss level, the stop loss order might be executed at a much worse price than intended, causing higher losses than initially expected.

Other traders favour an approach that requires their intervention when certain indicators, particularly the *delta* of the option contract, suggest it. *Delta* primarily measures the sensitivity of the option's price to the underlying asset's price changes, but it is also used by many professional traders to statistically predict the likelihood of an option expiring in-the-money. Traders following this approach stay in the trade until the delta indicates a high risk of the option expiring in-the-money. At this point, they close the trade and immediately open a new one at a delta that meets their risk requirements, thereby mitigating assignment costs while maintaining an acceptable level of profit.

I don't prefer this approach, which can also use other indicators besides delta because it requires constant trade monitoring. This doesn't align with my needs, as I don't want to spend most of my time in front of my laptop checking on my trades. Additionally, there is a real risk that corrective measures of this type may be needed more than once in a trading week. This, combined with the specific nature of index options, can significantly harm the profitability of the strategy and yield less advantageous results than those achievable without such measures.

Another potential corrective action, often favored by traders, is the so-called "*rollover*" of the trade. This means closing the current trade by buying back the put option you initially sold and selling the protective put you had previously bought, then re-executing the trade for the same expiration date but at a lower strike price, or for the following week at the same or a lower strike price.

Despite its popularity, I don't recommend this approach. The reason is that rolling over the trade often requires you to spend almost as much as you would have lost if you simply let the trade run its course. For example, with an index option, this could mean paying nearly $1,000. When you repeat the trade at a lower strike price for the same expiration, the premium you collect will likely be much lower—around $200—compared to the original premium you received earlier in the week.

If you do the calculations, you may find that with this approach, you could earn about $500 in total, including approximately $300 from the initial trade, which would leave you with a net loss of around $450–500. Plus, you will still be exposed to the risk of further market declines. If the market continues to drop and the new trade also fails, your losses could end up being even larger than they would have been originally.

Even if you roll the trade to the next week, the premium you receive might be similar or slightly higher, but it still won't be enough to fully cover your losses. Additionally, you'll remain vulnerable to the risk of another assignment, which could be likely if market conditions aren't favourable for implementing the strategy that week (meaning the 10-DMA and the 20-DMA are above the SPX line), making the situation even more precarious. Indeed, it is well known that losing trades often occur in clusters, typically during market pullback or correction periods. You may be forced to roll the trade over again to the following week, suffering additional losses. In the end, it's a lot of effort and stress for limited benefit. I'd rather take the loss and move on, knowing that in the long term, the strategy will still be very profitable for me.

After a few years of implementing this strategy, I can say with great confidence that, based on my experience and historical data analysis, the best way to handle situations where the trade goes against you when using the Slick strategy is to do nothing. Instead of focusing on complex techniques that may offer minimal benefit, cause stress, and lead to mistakes that can result in additional losses, it is wiser to mentally prepare yourself to accept that not all trades will be successful. Learn to manage downturns by trusting in the long-term robustness of your strategy.

In the end, rather than pursuing any corrective actions, it would be far more effective to reduce the risk of execution mistakes by developing a detailed strategy implementation plan that outlines all your key trading decisions. You should also make a firm commitment to strictly adhere to this plan and take a moment every Monday morning to review it before logging into your broker account and starting your trading.

4. The Final Touch

In this chapter, after going through the Slick strategy in detail, I want to talk about the problems that non-expert traders often encounter. These problems are usually overlooked in specialized books because professional traders assume everyone already knows this stuff. My goal is to save you from having to figure things out the hard way, like I did, because making mistakes in this business can be expensive.

4.1 Dealing with your emotions

Warren Buffet is used to say that the most important quality for an investor is temperament, not intellect. Investing and trading are inherently emotional activities. The ability to control emotions is a critical skill that can significantly impact an individual's financial success.

The fluctuation of market prices can evoke strong psychological responses. For instance, when markets are soaring, investors may feel euphoria and a sense of invincibility, leading to overconfidence and excessive risk-taking. Conversely, during market downturns, fear and panic can set in, causing investors to make hasty decisions, such as selling at a loss. These emotional reactions are often counterproductive and can derail even a well-thought-out trading strategy like the Slick one.

How your emotions can impact the execution of the Slick strategy

Emotions can cloud judgment and lead to impulsive actions that are not aligned with your strategy. Fortunately, the Slick strategy is quite simple and mechanical, requiring few decisions. However, its implementation is not immune to some of the typical emotional mistakes. Two of the most common emotional pitfalls are related to greed and fear:

1. **Greed**: Greed can generally drive you to chase high-risk opportunities or hold onto winning positions for too long, hoping for even greater gains. In the Slick strategy, this may result in a decision to significantly increase the number of option contracts sold because the strategy is currently yielding great results, and you are aiming for even greater profits. However, winning trades don't last forever, and you may risk facing losses greater than you're prepared to tolerate.

   For example, if you decided to implement the strategy by selling five option contracts, after a month of successful trades, you may have cashed in around $6,000. Following the euphoria from such gains, you might decide to triple your investment, disregarding all your previous carefully thought-out considerations that led to the decision to sell five option contracts for the strategy implementation. As a result, you are now selling fifteen option contracts. Unfortunately, the following trade turns out to be a loss. Because you tripled your investment, your losses may now amount to around $10,000, offsetting all your previous gains and generating a net loss of about $4,000. Of course, by sticking to the strategy, you will be able to recover from the loss, but are you ready to accept and digest such a significant setback right away? Are you confident that fear won't lead you to abandon the strategy or double the number of contracts you sell next week in a rush to recover your losses, which would significantly increase your risk? If you're uncertain about your ability to handle this, it might be wiser to play it safe, limit the amount at risk, and always stick to your initial trading plan.

2. **Fear:** Fear typically can cause investors and traders to sell assets prematurely, often at a loss. This behavior is commonly observed during market corrections or bear markets. Instead of sticking to a rational plan, fear-driven investors may liquidate their portfolios to avoid further losses, potentially missing out on subsequent recoveries. This fully applies to investors trading the Slick strategy as well. When market trends change, and you experience two consecutive losses, fear can easily start to mount.

Because of that, when deciding how many option contracts you are going to sell per week, besides your financial capacity and your profit objective, which I previously discussed, there is another criterion that you need to consider very carefully: how much you can emotionally afford to lose. This is no less important than your financial capacity. I am not talking about how much you can financially bear; you may have the financial capacity to absorb a loss of $20,000 in a week when your trade is unsuccessful, but whether you can stomach such a loss is a completely different matter. Instead of getting blinded by potential profits, you need to honestly ask yourself whether you are emotionally capable, beyond your financial capacity, of dealing with the impact of such a potential loss. If you do not feel ready for that, then you should not risk such an amount because this is a situation that can and will happen, and it may lead you to make poor decisions that will inevitably cause execution errors. As I have already said, mistakes in this business can be very costly. You might decide to stop trading the strategy, which could hinder your ability to recover from the loss and make profits in the future.

There are several existing strategies for emotional control. While this is not the purpose of this book, I recommend that if you do not feel 100% ready or lack experience with emotional bias, you should start trading the Slick strategy with a smaller amount. Even one option contract could be sufficient. Make some profits and allow your confidence in the strategy to grow before you increase your investment. Above all, it is critical to have a well-defined investment plan where you commit to proper strategy implementation for at least a full cycle of 52 weeks. For this purpose, it is advisable to deposit more funds into your broker account than required for the weekly execution of the trading, accounting for possible consecutive losses. This approach avoids the need to add money to the account if the profits obtained up to that point cannot fully cover incurred losses, ensuring the continued execution of the strategy.

Finally, an adequate period of paper trading can greatly enhance your familiarity with the strategy, boosting your confidence in it. However, the minimum duration of the paper trading period should be clearly established in your trading plan to avoid the temptation, if things are going well, to prematurely switch to real money out of euphoria, potentially doing so before you're fully ready.

4.2 Dos and Don'ts

I am sure you are familiar with the saying, *"The devil is in the details."* There is always some truth in this adage. In this section, I aim to provide you with my final recommendations, often related to minor aspects of the strategy implementation but which may still impact its successful outcome. These are not actions you *must take* or must avoid. They are merely suggestions that, if followed, can enhance the smooth implementation of the strategy. They are all based on the analysis of historical market data or personal experience gained through trial and error. Some recommendations may sound like a repetition of previous instructions. This is intentional because I felt the message needed to be sufficiently emphasized.

DOs

- Commit to executing the Slick strategy for at least a full cycle of 52 weeks.
- Use a dedicated broker account for strategy implementation. If you already have an account, consider opening a new one, as most brokers allow for multiple accounts. Managing the strategy separately from your other investments is highly recommended. It's challenging to accurately monitor the strategy's performance if the account is used for multiple investments. Additionally, if you hold a margin account, downturns in other investments could prevent you from maintaining the minimum funds required for the strategy, potentially hindering its effectiveness.
- Set investment objectives that are compatible with your financial capacity.
- Use a reliable online service that offers real-time market data, including simple charts, a market calendar, and basic market news. I prefer *MarketWatch.com* because it easily provides all of these features in one place. I dislike navigating between multiple websites to gather the necessary information. These activities, while important for the proper execution of the Slick strategy, should take no more than 5 minutes.
- Practice the strategy through paper trading until you're

confident enough to use real money. Break down the process step by step—from starting a trade to monitoring and potentially closing it. Make sure you thoroughly understand each step, along with all the associated risks, details, and possible alternatives, before moving forward.

- Do not let fear drive your decisions. If you face a series of negative trades, remain confident in the robustness of the strategy. If the loss of a trade is determined by an execution error, learn from the lesson and implement effective mechanisms to avoid repeating the same mistake. In any case, do not change your trading strategy plan before the relevant 52-week cycle is completed.

- If possible, deposit three times the amount your broker requires to execute the strategy based on the number of option contracts you plan to sell each week. This precaution helps you avoid needing to add funds to your broker account in case of a series of unsuccessful trades that result in losses not fully offset by previous gains. Additionally, this approach can help you manage your emotions, reducing the risk of abandoning the strategy instead of depositing additional funds.

- Watch the step-by-step video guide on the strategy implementation very carefully.

Don'ts

- Avoid monitoring the trade through your broker account, as it can be too tempting to take actions that may lead to execution errors, especially if the trade is moving against you. Instead, use a separate online service like MarketWatch.com to access real-time data. It will give you time to reflect before you access your account and take action.

- Do not give too much importance to market news. Big investors, market experts, and analysts often predict an imminent market crash, and like a broken watch is right at least twice a day, they may also be right once in a while. However, this is much less frequent than their predictions.

- Do not set profit objectives that involve potential weekly losses you are not fully and unquestionably prepared to handle.
- Do not become overconfident if you achieve significant gains. Especially, avoid changing your trading strategy before the relevant 52-week cycle is completed.
- If you decide to sell more than one option contract per week, do not sell some at a strike price 30 points below the market level according to the strategy rules, and others at a different strike price for diversification. This approach carries the concrete risk that the gains from some option contracts could be completely offset by the losses from others.
- Do not adjust the number of option contracts sold each week based on perceived risk; simply adhere to the strategy's rules. This is your best and safest bet. While risk management is essential, over-managing the strategy by increasing or decreasing the number of contracts based on gut feelings or fear of potential losses could cause you to miss out on profitable trades. This can erode the overall profitability of your strategy and reduce its effectiveness.
- If you determine that the conditions for the early close of your trades are met, close all of them. Do not close only some contracts while leaving others open. If the decision to close is valid, it should apply to all your ongoing trades.
- When a trade is moving against you, do not attempt to recover potential losses by initiating a new trade in the middle of the trading week. This tactic can lead to even greater losses, as the negative market trend might persist, resulting in your new option contract also ending up in-the-money.
- On the last day of the trading week, if your trade is successful but the conditions for an early close do not apply, you may be

tempted to close it anyway for a small gain out of fear that a minor downturn could lead to a loss. Don't do that. In the long run, this approach may significantly harm the profitability of your strategy. If you cannot emotionally manage the risk of a potential loss, reduce the number of contracts sold to bring your risk to a level you can handle.

- Do not pause the strategy execution for reasons other than those specified by the strategy rules outlined in this book. Attempting to predict when the strategy might be unsuccessful is akin to trying to time the market. It's simply ineffective. Mathematically, given that you should execute an average of 43 trades per year, with only 5 typically resulting in losses, your chances of accurately predicting an unsuccessful week are just slightly above 10%. In nearly 90% of cases, you'd be wrong and miss out on potential profits.

- Do not execute the strategy when, according to its rules, it should be paused. Even if you strongly believe the trade will be successful, the risk is too high. In the long run, not adhering to this rule can harm the strategy's profitability.

- Do not chase higher premiums, as this may increase the risk (i.e., ending up selling the put at less than 30 points below the market level) or delay the trade initiation (i.e., waiting too long for an order with a higher premium to be executed), which can also result in greater risk. Anything in the range of $280-$340 is acceptable.

4.3 How to secure a regular monthly income

At this point, I am confident that I have sufficiently demonstrated how the Slick strategy can lead you to financial independence in *little* time, even if you have *little* market experience, **little** technical skills, **little** money to invest, and **little** time to dedicate to trading. There is one thing I mentioned in my preamble that I still need to explain: *how to secure a regular monthly income through the strategy.* In fact, I have mentioned more than once that, inevitably, there will be losses. In some unlikely but still possible cases, there could even be a series of unsuccessful trades. It's clear that when losses occur, it may be difficult or even impossible to withdraw your regular monthly income, as the funds may not be available.

> *So, how can I be confident that securing a regular monthly income is possible with the Slick strategy?*

It's possible, but I must admit there's a caveat: You need to wait for one year of successful strategy implementation before you can start receiving your monthly check.

> *How does that work?*

Let me explain what I did to achieve that. I started developing my strategy towards the end of 2021, with most of the design completed during 2022. I paper traded the strategy for a few months during the summer of that year. Eventually, I started implementing the strategy at the beginning of October 2022. Initially, I still went through a period of trial and error, which allowed me to refine the strategy design and procedures. I made some 12-13 trades, with 3 to 4 unsuccessful trades. I did not make any money, but I also did not incur any losses. At the end of 2022, my balance was just around $1,000 higher than it was when I started the strategy's implementation. At the beginning of 2023, I was ready. I developed my trading plan. In particular, I decided to execute the strategy for the whole year, selling ten option contracts. I opened a dedicated account with my broker to execute the strategy and deposited $20,000, which is more than three times the amount at risk to implement the strategy. I also made another crucial decision: I committed to not withdrawing any proceeds for the entire year. With these guidelines in place, I proceeded to implement the strategy, and my final performance at the end of 2023 is detailed in the table below:

Trading Week	No of Option contracts	Non-trading Weeks	Trades won	Trades Lost	Total Premium	Total Losses	Annual Balance
52	10	13	33	6	91,450.00	42,000.00	49,450.00

These results amounted to a bit more than $4,000 per month. By the end of the year, my brokerage account had almost $70,000. Having decided earlier that $3,000 would be a reasonable monthly withdrawal for me, I could now confidently withdraw this amount every month, regardless of the strategy's performance in any subsequent month.

In full disclosure, I decided to wait until the end of June 2024 to withdraw any funds, allowing the strategy's proceeds to accumulate in my brokerage account. I made this decision to ensure coverage for my monthly withdrawals even in the event of a prolonged bearish period, similar to what occurred in 2022.

I am not sure that the same criteria can apply to you. You may set a different monthly amount to withdraw or choose a different number of option contracts to sell each week. Additionally, when you start the strategy implementation, the market conditions may differ from those of 2023, which was a very bullish year but also extremely volatile. You could have a better year than 2023, with fewer pauses in the strategy than I experienced, allowing you to potentially earn more than I did with the same level of investment. But of course, you may also face a bearish period and need more time to accumulate the funds required to cover your monthly income withdrawals. In any case, I am confident that with this approach, sooner or later, you will reach your goals. You will certainly do so much earlier than with other standard investment techniques, which are likely more complex, require more money to invest, involve higher risk, and demand much more time for their implementation.

5.0 SPX Strategy Backtesting Data Analysis

2014-2023 and AI validation

By presenting the historical market data, I aim to demonstrate the strategy's consistency and reliability across various market conditions encompassing volatility phases and economic cycles. This historical perspective serves to corroborate the validity of the strategy and its robustness, showing how it has performed in real-world scenarios over an extended period. The historical performance of the Slick strategy should not be underestimated. Consider this: Warren Buffett is widely admired, with millions of investors replicating his investments, not just because of his charm but due to his proven track record. While there's no guarantee he will replicate past success, the prevailing expectation is that history will repeat itself, and this time won't be any different. Past performance matters, and it matters a lot. The Slick strategy's backtesting results are undeniably impressive.

Furthermore, I included AI validation in this chapter to assess the accuracy of my assumptions, calculations, and analysis regarding the strategy's low risk and high profitability, while also providing an additional layer of scrutiny. Although I acknowledge the limitations of using AI for such validation, I believe it can serve as a complementary tool to offer a well-rounded evaluation of the strategy's potential effectiveness. The AI's perspective, while not a definitive measure, acts as a secondary checkpoint that can be valuable when cross-referenced with historical performance data. This dual approach, combining historical analysis with AI validation, is designed to enhance confidence in the strategy's quality and adaptability for future applications.

5.1 Summary Tables of the Slick Strategy's Performance

In this chapter, you will find comprehensive summary tables of the Slick strategy's performance over the period 2014-2023, based on historical market data and the assumption of selling 10 option contracts per week. The calculation does not include the commission fee possibly charged by the broker and any payable taxes. The premiums are calculated based on recurring market prices for similar trades. All financial data are presented in US dollars, as this is the currency used for executing the strategy. For those holding funds in other currencies, I recommend using WISE for currency conversion. WISE offers among the best market rates with minimal fees, which are much more competitive than those charged by most brokers. Most importantly, if you have an account with Interactive Brokers, you can connect it to your Wise account, allowing you to transfer funds instantly and directly between the two accounts.

Year	Trading Week	Non-trading Weeks	Trades won	Trades Lost	Total Premium***	Total Losses	Annual Balance
2023	52	13	33	6	99,000	42,000	57,000
2022	52	0	5	3	15,000	21,000	- 6,000
2021	52	5	39	8	117,000	56,000	61,000
2020	53	13	32*	7	93,080	49,000	44,080
2019	52	6	42	4	126,000	28,000	98,000
2018	52	23	27	2	81,000	14,000	67,000
2017	52	-	50	2**	150,000	5,240	144,760
2016	52	7	41	4	123,000	28,000	95,000
2015	53	13	34	6**	102,000	4,170	97,830
2014	53	6	41*	6**	122,200	40,570	81,630

*Two trades only partially successful.
**One trade only partially unsuccessful.
***Calculated pre-taxes, based on recurring market prices for the same type of trade.

	Total Premium	Total Losses	Balance
Annual Average	102,828	28,798	74,030
Grand total	1,028,280	287,980	740,300
Monthly Average Income			6,169

GRAND TOTAL	Trading Week	Non-trading Weeks	Trades won	Trades Lost	Total Premium	Total Losses	Total Balance
	523	86	344	48	1,028,280	287,980	740,300

ANNUAL AVERAGE	Trading Week	Non-trading Weeks*	Trades won	Trades Lost	Total Premium	Total Losses	Average Balance
	52	8.6	38.2	5.3	102,828	28,798	74,030

*Excluding 2022

Best year	2017	Bullish period	7
Worse year	2022	Bearish period	3
Highest Annual Income	144,760	Bullish period duration (in months)	100
Lowest Annual Income	44,080	Bearish period duration (in months)	20
Average Capital invested per week	7,000	Average loss profit option contract	300
Maximum loss in a calendar year	-6,000	Average loss per option contract	700

5.2 AI Validation

I tested my strategy using ChatGPT-4 from OpenAI, which is considered one of the best AI models for complex tasks. After explaining in detail the characteristics and implementation modalities of the Slick strategy to the AI model and uploading all the backtesting data, this is the response I received:

Thank you for sharing the comprehensive implementation details of the Slick strategy. You've covered everything from how to initiate the trade, monitor it, and when to close it, to possible corrective actions and their effectiveness. This level of detail will undoubtedly help anyone trying to execute the strategy successfully.

If you're ready to ask your questions or share more information, feel free to proceed. I'm here to assist with any further clarifications or next steps.

Next, I posed a straightforward question, asking for feedback on the overall strategy.

> So, based on what you have learned about the Slick Strategy what is your final view on it?

The Slick Strategy is a well-thought-out and data-driven approach to options trading that balances profitability with risk management. Its use of historical market data and disciplined execution rules, particularly the incorporation of the 10-day, 20-day, and 200-day moving averages, demonstrates a strong commitment to minimizing risk during volatile periods. This focus on avoiding trades when market conditions are unfavorable helps protect against significant losses, which is a key strength of the strategy.

The backtesting results over the past decade show that the strategy can yield consistent profits, even in challenging years. While there were some periods of underperformance, the overall approach of pausing trades during high-risk periods and leveraging statistical data has proven effective in preserving capital and maintaining profitability.

In summary, the Slick Strategy is a solid and methodical trading approach that offers a good balance between risk and reward. It is particularly suitable for traders who prefer a structured, rule-based strategy with a strong focus on risk management. As with any trading strategy, ongoing monitoring and adherence to the established rules are essential to sustaining long-term success.

Beyond the positive feedback received, I want to emphasize that even the AI underscored the critical need to follow the strategy's rules precisely to achieve the desired outcomes. That was my challenge, and now it's yours as well. However, with the guidance provided in this book, I'm confident you'll succeed.

5.3 Backtesting Historical Market Data

Naturally, it's crucial that you can also verify the data directly. Hence, the historical market data is provided below, organized in reverse order from 2023 to 2014, categorized by year and week.

Please note that the negative red numbers in the 'Outcome' column represent unsuccessful instances of the strategy. All dates in **bold** indicate periods when the strategy should have been paused, and therefore, trades during these times should not be included in profitability calculations. However, the value of the put sold and the potential trade outcomes are still provided for those weeks when trading should have been paused, allowing for a comprehensive evaluation of the potential benefits and drawbacks of using the 10- and 20-day Moving Average Lines. Furthermore, the value of the 'Put Sold' for all trades has not been rounded to the nearest purchasable level, except when necessary to determine the trade's success.

In case you would like to analyze the historical data yourself, you can download the spreadsheet using the QR code below:

Below you can also find the QR code to access the Video Guide for the Step-by-Step strategy implementation:

With this information, data, and tools at your disposal, I am confident that you are fully equipped to begin implementing the **Slick strategy** effectively and could soon see your account growing week by week.

Thank you so much for making it this far!

I greatly appreciate the time you took to read my book. As a small independent publisher, your support means the world to me, and I hope I am giving something back to you by making a difference in your investing journey.

If you have a few more seconds, I would deeply appreciate to hear your honest feedback on the platform you used to make your purchase. Your review can do wonders for the book, and I'd love hearing about your experience with it.

Thank you very much!

Year 2023

Week	Date	Open	Close	Put Sold	Outcome
1	1/2/23	3853.29	3895.08	3825	70.08
2	1/9/23	3910.82	3999.09	3881	118.27
3	1/16/23	3999.28	3972.61	3969	3.33
4	1/23/23	3978.14	4070.56	3948	122.42
5	1/30/23	4049.27	4136.48	4019	117.21
6	2/6/23	4119.57	4090.46	4090	0.89
7	2/13/23	4096.62	4079.09	4067	12.47
8	2/20/23	4052.35	3970.04	4022	-52.31
9	2/27/23	3992.36	4045.64	3962	83.28
10	3/6/23	4055.15	3861.59	4025	-163.56
11	3/13/23	3835.12	3916.64	3805	111.52
12	3/20/23	3917.47	3970.99	3887	83.52
13	3/27/23	3982.93	4109.31	3953	156.38
14	4/3/23	4102.20	4105.02	4072	32.82
15	4/10/23	4085.20	4137.64	4055	82.44
16	4/17/23	4137.17	4133.52	4107	26.35
17	4/24/23	4132.07	4169.48	4102	67.41
18	5/1/23	4166.79	4136.25	4135	1.25
19	5/8/23	4136.98	4124.08	4107	17.10
20	5/15/23	4126.65	4191.98	4097	95.33
21	5/22/23	4190.78	4205.45	4161	44.67
22	5/29/23	4226.71	4282.37	4197	85.66
23	6/5/23	4282.99	4298.86	4253	45.87
24	6/12/23	4308.32	4409.59	4278	131.27
25	6/19/23	4396.11	4348.33	4366	-17.78
26	6/26/23	4344.84	4450.38	4315	135.54
27	7/3/23	4450.48	4398.95	4420	-21.53
28	7/10/23	4394.23	4505.42	4364	141.19
29	7/17/23	4508.86	4536.34	4479	57.48
30	7/24/23	4543.39	4582.23	4513	68.84
31	7/31/23	4584.82	4478.03	4555	-76.79
32	8/7/23	4491.58	4464.05	4462	2.47
33	8/14/23	4458.13	4369.71	4428	-58.42
34	8/21/23	4380.28	4405.71	4350	55.43
35	8/28/23	4426.03	4515.77	4396	119.74
36	9/4/23	4510.06	4457.49	4480	-22.57
37	9/11/23	4480.98	4450.32	4450	0.32
38	9/18/23	4445.13	4320.06	4415	-95.07
39	9/25/23	4310.62	4288.05	4281	7.43
40	10/2/23	4284.52	4308.50	4255	53.98
41	10/9/23	4289.02	4327.78	4259	68.76
42	10/16/23	4342.37	4224.16	4312	-88.21
43	10/23/23	4210.40	4117.37	4180	-63.03
44	10/30/23	4139.39	4358.34	4109	248.95
45	11/6/23	4364.27	4415.24	4334	80.97
46	11/13/23	4406.66	4514.02	4377	137.36
47	11/20/23	4511.70	4559.34	4482	77.64
48	11/27/23	4554.86	4594.63	4525	69.77
49	12/4/23	4564.37	4604.37	4534	70.00
50	12/11/23	4593.39	4719.19	4563	155.80
51	12/18/23	4725.58	4754.63	4696	59.05
52	12/25/23	4758.86	4783.35	4729	54.49

Year 2022

Week	Date	Open	Close	Put Sold	Outcome
1	1/3/22	4778.14	4677.03	4748	-71.11
2	1/10/22	4655.34	4662.85	4625	37.51
3	1/17/22	4632.24	4397.94	4602	-204.30
4	1/24/22	4356.32	4431.85	4326	105.53
5	1/31/22	4431.79	4500.53	4402	98.74
6	2/7/22	4505.75	4418.64	4476	-57.11
7	2/14/22	4412.61	4348.87	4383	-33.74
8	2/21/22	4332.74	4384.65	4303	81.91
9	2/28/22	4354.17	4328.87	4324	4.70
10	3/7/22	4327.01	4204.31	4297	-92.70
11	3/14/22	4202.75	4463.12	4173	290.37
12	3/21/22	4462.40	4543.06	4432	110.66
13	3/28/22	4541.09	4545.86	4511	34.77
14	4/4/22	4547.97	4488.28	4518	-29.69
15	4/11/22	4462.64	4392.59	4433	-40.05
16	4/18/22	4385.63	4271.78	4356	-83.85
17	4/25/22	4255.34	4131.93	4225	-93.41
18	5/2/22	4130.61	4123.34	4101	22.73
19	5/9/22	4081.27	4023.89	4051	-27.38
20	5/16/22	4013.02	3901.36	3983	-81.66
21	5/23/22	3919.42	4158.24	3889	268.82
22	5/30/22	4151.09	4108.54	4121	-12.55
23	6/6/22	4134.72	3900.86	4105	-203.86
24	6/13/22	3838.15	3674.84	3808	-133.31
25	6/20/22	3715.31	3911.74	3685	226.43
26	6/27/22	3920.76	3825.33	3891	-65.43
27	7/4/22	3792.61	3899.38	3763	136.77
28	7/11/22	3880.94	3863.16	3851	12.22
29	7/18/22	3883.79	3961.63	3854	107.84
30	7/25/22	3965.72	4130.29	3936	194.57
31	8/1/22	4112.38	4145.19	4082	62.81
32	8/8/22	4155.93	4280.15	4126	154.22
33	8/15/22	4269.37	4228.48	4239	-10.89
34	8/22/22	4195.08	4057.66	4165	-107.42
35	8/29/22	4034.58	3924.26	4005	-80.32
36	9/5/22	3930.89	4067.36	3901	166.47
37	9/12/22	4083.67	3873.33	4054	-180.34
38	9/19/22	3849.91	3693.23	3820	-126.68
39	9/26/22	3682.72	3585.62	3653	-67.10
40	10/3/22	3609.78	3639.66	3580	59.88
41	10/10/22	3647.51	3583.07	3618	-34.44
42	10/17/22	3638.65	3752.75	3609	144.10
43	10/24/22	3762.01	3901.06	3732	169.05
44	10/31/22	3881.85	3770.55	3852	-81.30
45	11/7/22	3780.71	3992.93	3751	242.22
46	11/14/22	3977.97	3965.34	3948	17.37
47	11/21/22	3956.23	4026.12	3926	99.89
48	11/28/22	4005.36	4071.70	3975	96.34
49	12/5/22	4052.02	3934.38	4022	-87.64
50	12/12/22	3939.29	3852.36	3909	-56.93
51	12/19/22	3853.79	3844.82	3824	21.03
52	12/26/22	3843.34	3849.28	3813	35.94

Year 2021

Week	Date	Open	Close	Put Sold	Outcome
1	1/1/21	3764.61	3803.79	3735	68.79
2	1/8/21	3815.05	3795.54	3785	10.54
3	1/15/21	3788.73	3853.07	3759	94.07
4	1/22/21	3844.24	3787.38	3814	-26.62
5	1/29/21	3778.05	3871.74	3748	123.74
6	2/5/21	3878.30	3916.38	3848	68.38
7	2/12/21	3911.65	3913.97	3882	31.97
8	2/19/21	3921.16	3829.34	3891	-61.66
11	3/12/21	3924.52	3915.46	3895	20.46
12	3/19/21	3913.14	3909.52	3883	26.52
13	3/26/21	3917.12	4019.87	3887	132.87
14	4/2/21	4034.44	4097.17	4004	93.17
15	4/9/21	4096.11	4170.42	4066	104.42
16	4/16/21	4174.14	4134.98	4145	-10.02
17	4/23/21	4138.78	4211.47	4109	102.47
18	4/30/21	4198.10	4201.62	4168	33.62
19	5/7/21	4210.34	4112.50	4180	-67.50
21	5/21/21	4168.61	4200.88	4139	61.88
22	5/28/21	4210.77	4192.85	4181	11.85
23	6/4/21	4206.05	4239.18	4176	63.18
24	6/11/21	4242.90	4221.86	4213	8.86
25	6/18/21	4204.78	4266.49	4175	91.49
26	6/25/21	4274.45	4319.94	4244	75.94
27	7/2/21	4326.60	4320.82	4297	23.82
28	7/9/21	4329.38	4360.03	4299	61.03
29	7/16/21	4367.43	4367.48	4337	30.48
30	7/23/21	4381.20	4419.15	4351	68.15
31	7/30/21	4395.12	4429.10	4365	64.10
32	8/6/21	4429.07	4460.83	4399	61.83
33	8/13/21	4464.84	4405.80	4435	-29.20
34	8/20/21	4410.56	4470.00	4381	89.00
35	8/27/21	4474.10	4536.95	4444	92.95
36	9/3/21	4532.42	4493.28	4505	-11.72
42	10/15/21	4447.69	4549.78	4418	131.78
43	10/22/21	4546.12	4596.42	4516	80.42
44	10/29/21	4572.87	4680.06	4543	137.06
45	11/5/21	4699.26	4649.27	4669	-19.73
46	11/12/21	4655.24	4704.54	4625	79.54
47	11/19/21	4708.44	4701.46	4678	23.46
48	11/26/21	4664.63	4577.10	4635	-57.90
49	12/3/21	4589.49	4667.45	4559	108.45
50	12/10/21	4687.64	4668.67	4658	10.67
51	12/17/21	4652.50	4725.79	4623	102.79
52	12/24/21	4733.99	4778.73	4704	74.73

Year 2020

Week	Date	Open	Close	Put Sold	Outcome
1	12/30/19	3240.09	3234.85	3210	24.76
2	1/6/20	3217.55	3265.35	3188	77.80
3	1/13/20	3271.13	3329.62	3241	88.49
4	1/20/20	3321.03	3295.47	3291	4.44
5	1/27/20	3247.16	3225.52	3217	8.36
6	2/3/20	3235.66	3327.71	3206	122.05
7	2/10/20	3318.28	3380.16	3288	91.88
8	2/17/20	3369.04	3337.75	3340	-2.25
9	2/24/20	3257.61	2954.22	3228	-273.39
10	3/2/20	2974.28	2972.37	2944	28.09
11	3/9/20	2863.89	2711.02	2834	-122.87
12	3/16/20	2508.59	2304.92	2479	-173.67
13	3/23/20	2290.71	2541.47	2261	280.76
14	3/30/20	2558.98	2488.65	2529	-40.33
15	4/6/20	2578.28	2789.82	2548	241.54
16	4/13/20	2782.46	2874.56	2752	122.10
17	4/20/20	2845.62	2836.74	2816	21.12
18	4/27/20	2854.65	2830.71	2825	6.06
19	5/4/20	2815.01	2929.80	2785	144.79
20	5/11/20	2915.46	2863.70	2885	-21.76
21	5/18/20	2913.86	2955.45	2884	71.59
22	5/25/20	3004.08	3044.31	2974	70.23
23	6/1/20	3038.78	3193.93	3009	185.15
24	6/8/20	3199.92	3041.31	3170	-128.61
25	6/15/20	2993.76	3097.74	2964	133.98
26	6/22/20	3094.42	3009.05	3064	-55.37
27	6/29/20	3018.59	3130.01	2989	141.42
28	7/6/20	3155.29	3185.04	3125	59.75
29	7/13/20	3205.08	3224.73	3175	49.65
30	7/20/20	3224.29	3215.63	3194	21.34
31	7/27/20	3219.84	3271.12	3190	81.28
32	8/3/20	3288.26	3351.28	3258	93.02
33	8/10/20	3356.04	3372.85	3326	46.81
34	8/17/20	3380.86	3397.16	3351	46.30
35	8/24/20	3418.09	3508.01	3388	119.92
36	8/31/20	3509.73	3426.96	3480	-52.77
37	9/7/20	3371.88	3340.97	3345	-4.03
38	9/14/20	3363.56	3319.47	3334	-14.09
39	9/21/20	3285.57	3298.46	3256	42.89
40	9/28/20	3333.90	3348.42	3304	44.52
41	10/5/20	3367.27	3477.14	3337	139.87
42	10/12/20	3500.02	3483.81	3470	13.79
43	10/19/20	3493.66	3465.39	3464	1.73
44	10/26/20	3441.42	3269.96	3411	-141.46
45	11/2/20	3296.20	3509.44	3266	243.24
46	11/9/20	3583.04	3585.15	3553	32.11
47	11/16/20	3600.16	3557.54	3570	-12.62
48	11/23/20	3566.82	3638.35	3537	101.53
49	11/30/20	3631.18	3699.12	3604	94.94
50	12/7/20	3694.73	3663.46	3665	-1.27
51	12/14/20	3675.27	3709.41	3645	64.14
52	12/21/20	3684.28	3703.06	3654	48.78
53	12/28/20	3723.03	3756.07	3693	63.04

Year 2019

Week	Date	Open	Close	Put Sold	Outcome
1	12/31/18	2498.94	2531.94	2469	63.00
2	1/7/19	2535.61	2596.26	2506	90.65
3	1/14/19	2580.31	2670.71	2550	120.40
4	1/21/19	2657.88	2664.76	2628	36.88
5	1/28/19	2644.97	2706.53	2615	91.56
6	2/4/19	2706.49	2707.88	2676	31.39
7	2/11/19	2712.40	2775.60	2682	93.20
8	2/18/19	2769.28	2792.67	2739	53.39
9	2/25/19	2804.35	2803.69	2774	29.34
10	3/4/19	2814.37	2743.07	2784	-41.30
11	3/11/19	2747.61	2822.48	2718	104.87
12	3/18/19	2822.61	2800.71	2793	8.10
13	3/25/19	2796.01	2834.40	2766	68.39
14	4/1/19	2848.63	2892.74	2819	74.11
15	4/8/19	2888.46	2907.41	2858	48.95
16	4/15/19	2908.32	2905.03	2878	26.71
17	4/22/19	2898.78	2939.88	2869	71.10
18	4/29/19	2940.58	2945.64	2911	35.06
19	5/6/19	2908.89	2881.40	2879	2.51
20	5/13/19	2840.19	2859.53	2810	49.34
21	5/20/19	2841.94	2826.06	2812	14.12
22	5/27/19	2830.03	2752.06	2800	-47.97
23	6/3/19	2751.53	2873.34	2722	151.81
24	6/10/19	2885.83	2886.98	2856	31.15
25	6/17/19	2889.75	2950.46	2860	90.71
26	6/24/19	2951.42	2941.76	2921	20.34
27	7/1/19	2971.41	2990.41	2941	49.00
28	7/8/19	2979.77	3013.77	2950	64.00
29	7/15/19	3017.80	2976.61	2988	-11.19
30	7/22/19	2981.93	3025.86	2952	73.93
31	7/29/19	3024.47	2932.05	2994	-62.42
32	8/5/19	2898.07	2918.65	2868	50.58
33	8/12/19	2907.07	2888.68	2877	11.61
34	8/19/19	2913.48	2847.11	2883	-36.37
35	8/26/19	2866.70	2926.46	2837	89.76
36	9/2/19	2909.01	2978.71	2879	99.70
37	9/9/19	2988.43	3007.39	2958	48.96
38	9/16/19	2996.41	2992.07	2966	25.66
39	9/23/19	2983.50	2961.79	2954	8.29
40	9/30/19	2967.07	2952.01	2937	14.94
41	10/7/19	2944.23	2970.27	2914	56.04
42	10/14/19	2965.81	2986.20	2936	50.39
43	10/21/19	2996.48	3022.55	2966	56.07
44	10/28/19	3032.12	3066.91	3002	64.79
45	11/4/19	3078.96	3093.08	3049	44.12
46	11/11/19	3080.33	3120.46	3050	70.13
47	11/18/19	3117.91	3110.29	3088	22.38
48	11/25/19	3117.44	3140.98	3087	53.54
49	12/2/19	3143.85	3145.91	3114	32.06
50	12/9/19	3141.86	3168.80	3112	56.94
51	12/16/19	3183.63	3221.22	3154	67.59
52	12/23/19	3226.05	3239.91	3196	43.86

Year 2018

Week	Date	Open	Close	Put Sold	Outcome
1	1/1/18	2683.73	2743.15	2654	89.42
2	1/8/18	2742.67	2786.24	2713	73.57
3	1/15/18	2798.96	2810.30	2769	41.34
4	1/22/18	2809.16	2872.87	2779	93.71
5	1/29/18	2867.23	2762.13	2837	-75.10
6	2/5/18	2741.06	2619.55	2711	-91.51
7	2/12/18	2636.75	2732.22	2607	125.47
8	2/19/18	2722.99	2747.30	2693	54.31
9	2/26/18	2757.37	2691.25	2727	-36.12
10	3/5/18	2681.06	2786.57	2651	135.51
11	3/12/18	2790.54	2752.01	2761	-8.53
12	3/19/18	2741.38	2588.26	2711	-123.12
13	3/26/18	2619.35	2640.87	2589	51.52
14	4/2/18	2633.45	2604.47	2603	1.02
15	4/9/18	2617.18	2656.30	2587	69.12
16	4/16/18	2670.10	2670.14	2640	30.04
17	4/23/18	2675.40	2669.91	2645	24.51
18	4/30/18	2682.51	2663.42	2653	10.91
19	5/7/18	2680.34	2727.72	2650	77.38
20	5/14/18	2738.47	2712.97	2710	2.97
21	5/21/18	2735.39	2721.33	2705	15.94
22	5/28/18	2705.11	2734.62	2675	59.51
23	6/4/18	2741.67	2779.03	2712	67.36
24	6/11/18	2780.18	2779.66	2750	29.48
25	6/18/18	2765.79	2754.88	2736	19.09
26	6/25/18	2742.94	2718.37	2713	5.43
27	7/2/18	2704.95	2759.82	2675	84.87
28	7/9/18	2775.62	2801.31	2746	55.69
29	7/16/18	2797.36	2801.83	2767	34.47
30	7/23/18	2799.17	2818.82	2769	49.65
31	7/30/18	2819.00	2840.35	2789	51.35
32	8/6/18	2840.29	2833.28	2810	22.99
33	8/13/18	2835.46	2850.13	2805	44.67
34	8/20/18	2853.93	2874.69	2824	50.76
35	8/27/18	2884.69	2901.52	2855	46.83
36	9/3/18	2896.96	2871.68	2870	1.68
37	9/10/18	2881.39	2904.98	2851	53.59
38	9/17/18	2903.83	2929.67	2874	55.84
39	9/24/18	2921.83	2913.98	2892	22.15
40	10/1/18	2926.29	2885.57	2896	-10.72
41	10/8/18	2877.53	2767.13	2848	-80.40
42	10/15/18	2763.83	2767.78	2734	33.95
43	10/22/18	2773.94	2658.69	2744	-85.25
44	10/29/18	2682.65	2723.06	2653	70.41
45	11/5/18	2726.37	2781.01	2696	84.64
46	11/12/18	2773.93	2736.27	2744	-7.66
47	11/19/18	2730.74	2632.56	2701	-68.18
48	11/26/18	2649.97	2760.17	2620	140.20
49	12/3/18	2790.50	2633.08	2761	-127.42
50	12/10/18	2630.86	2599.95	2600	-0.05
51	12/17/18	2590.75	2416.62	2561	-144.13
52	12/24/18	2400.56	2488.83	2371	118.27

Year 2017

Week	Date	Open	Close	Put Sold	Outcome
1	1/2/17	2251.57	2276.98	2222	55.41
2	1/9/17	2273.59	2274.64	2244	31.05
3	1/16/17	2269.14	2271.31	2239	32.17
4	1/23/17	2267.78	2294.69	2238	56.91
5	1/30/17	2286.01	2297.42	2256	41.41
6	2/6/17	2294.28	2316.10	2264	51.82
7	2/13/17	2321.72	2351.16	2292	59.44
8	2/20/17	2354.91	2367.34	2325	42.43
9	2/27/17	2365.23	2383.12	2335	47.89
10	3/6/17	2375.23	2372.60	2345	27.37
11	3/13/17	2371.56	2378.25	2342	36.69
12	3/20/17	2378.24	2343.98	2350	-6.02
13	3/27/17	2329.11	2362.72	2299	63.61
14	4/3/17	2362.34	2355.54	2332	23.20
15	4/10/17	2357.16	2328.95	2327	1.79
16	4/17/17	2332.62	2348.69	2303	46.07
17	4/24/17	2370.33	2384.20	2340	43.87
18	5/1/17	2388.50	2399.29	2359	40.79
19	5/8/17	2399.94	2390.90	2370	20.96
20	5/15/17	2393.98	2381.73	2364	17.75
21	5/22/17	2387.21	2415.82	2357	58.61
22	5/29/17	2411.67	2439.07	2382	57.40
23	6/5/17	2437.83	2431.77	2408	23.94
24	6/12/17	2425.88	2433.15	2396	37.27
25	6/19/17	2442.55	2438.30	2413	25.75
26	6/26/17	2443.32	2423.41	2413	10.09
27	7/3/17	2431.39	2425.18	2401	23.79
28	7/10/17	2424.51	2459.27	2395	64.76
29	7/17/17	2459.50	2472.54	2430	43.04
30	7/24/17	2472.04	2472.10	2442	30.06
31	7/31/17	2475.94	2476.83	2446	30.89
32	8/7/17	2477.14	2441.32	2447	-5.82
33	8/14/17	2454.96	2425.55	2425	0.59
34	8/21/17	2425.50	2443.05	2396	47.55
35	8/28/17	2447.35	2476.55	2417	59.20
36	9/4/17	2470.35	2461.43	2440	21.08
37	9/11/17	2474.52	2500.23	2445	55.71
38	9/18/17	2502.51	2502.22	2473	29.71
39	9/25/17	2499.39	2519.36	2469	49.97
40	10/2/17	2521.20	2549.33	2491	58.13
41	10/9/17	2551.39	2553.17	2521	31.78
42	10/16/17	2555.57	2575.21	2526	49.64
43	10/23/17	2578.08	2581.07	2548	32.99
44	10/30/17	2577.75	2587.84	2548	40.09
45	11/6/17	2587.47	2582.30	2557	24.83
46	11/13/17	2576.53	2578.85	2547	32.32
47	11/20/17	2579.49	2602.42	2549	52.93
48	11/27/17	2602.66	2642.22	2573	69.56
49	12/4/17	2657.19	2651.50	2627	24.31
50	12/11/17	2652.19	2675.81	2622	53.62
51	12/18/17	2685.92	2683.34	2656	27.42
52	12/25/17	2679.09	2687.54	2649	38.45

Year 2016

Week	Date	Open	Close	Put Sold	Outcome
1	1/4/16	2038.20	1922.03	2008	-86.17
2	1/11/16	1926.12	1880.33	1896	-15.79
3	1/18/16	1888.66	1906.90	1859	48.24
4	1/25/16	1906.28	1940.24	1876	63.96
5	2/1/16	1936.94	1880.05	1907	-26.89
6	2/8/16	1873.25	1864.78	1843	21.53
7	2/15/16	1871.44	1917.78	1841	76.34
8	2/22/16	1924.44	1948.05	1894	53.61
9	2/29/16	1947.13	1999.99	1917	82.86
10	3/7/16	1996.11	2022.19	1966	56.08
11	3/14/16	2019.27	2049.58	1989	60.31
12	3/21/16	2047.88	2035.94	2018	18.06
13	3/28/16	2037.89	2072.78	2008	64.89
14	4/4/16	2073.19	2047.60	2043	4.41
15	4/11/16	2050.23	2080.73	2020	60.50
16	4/18/16	2078.83	2091.58	2049	42.75
17	4/25/16	2089.37	2065.30	2059	5.93
18	5/2/16	2067.17	2057.14	2037	19.97
19	5/9/16	2057.55	2046.61	2028	19.06
20	5/16/16	2046.53	2052.32	2017	35.79
21	5/23/16	2052.23	2099.06	2022	76.83
22	5/30/16	2100.13	2099.13	2070	29.00
23	6/6/16	2100.83	2096.07	2071	25.24
24	6/13/16	2091.75	2071.22	2062	9.47
25	6/20/16	2075.58	2037.41	2046	-8.17
26	6/27/16	2031.45	2102.95	2001	101.50
27	7/4/16	2095.05	2129.90	2065	64.85
28	7/11/16	2131.72	2161.74	2102	60.02
29	7/18/16	2162.04	2175.03	2132	42.99
30	7/25/16	2173.71	2173.60	2144	29.89
31	8/1/16	2173.15	2182.87	2143	39.72
32	8/8/16	2183.76	2184.05	2154	30.29
33	8/15/16	2186.08	2183.87	2156	27.79
34	8/22/16	2181.58	2169.04	2152	17.46
35	8/29/16	2170.19	2179.98	2140	39.79
36	9/5/16	2181.61	2127.81	2152	-23.80
37	9/12/16	2120.86	2139.16	2091	48.30
38	9/19/16	2143.99	2164.69	2114	50.70
39	9/26/16	2158.54	2168.27	2129	39.73
40	10/3/16	2164.33	2153.74	2134	19.41
41	10/10/16	2160.39	2132.98	2130	2.59
42	10/17/16	2132.95	2141.16	2103	38.21
43	10/24/16	11/17/05	2126.41	2119	7.91
44	10/31/16	2129.78	2085.18	2100	-14.60
45	11/7/16	2100.59	2164.45	2071	93.86
46	11/14/16	2165.64	2181.90	2136	46.26
47	11/21/16	2186.43	2213.35	2156	56.92
48	11/28/16	2210.21	2191.95	2180	11.74
49	12/5/16	2200.65	2259.53	2171	88.88
50	12/12/16	2258.83	2258.07	2229	29.24
51	12/19/16	2259.24	2263.79	2229	34.55
52	12/26/16	2266.23	2249.26	2236	13.03

Year 2015

Week	Date	Open	Close	Put Sold	Outcome
1	12/29/14	2087.63	2058.20	2055	3.20
2	1/5/15	2054.44	2044.81	2024	20.37
3	1/12/15	2046.13	2019.42	2016	3.29
4	1/19/15	2020.76	2051.82	1991	61.06
5	1/26/15	2050.42	1994.99	2020	-25.43
6	2/2/15	1996.67	2055.47	1967	88.80
7	2/9/15	2053.47	2096.99	2023	73.52
8	2/16/15	2096.47	2110.30	2066	43.83
9	2/23/15	2109.83	2104.50	2080	24.67
10	3/2/15	2105.23	2071.26	2075	-3.97
11	3/9/15	2072.25	2053.40	2042	11.15
12	3/16/15	2055.35	2108.10	2025	82.75
13	3/23/15	2107.99	2061.02	2078	-16.97
14	3/30/15	2064.11	2066.96	2034	32.85
15	4/6/15	2064.87	2102.06	2035	67.19
16	4/13/15	2102.03	2081.18	2072	9.15
17	4/20/15	2084.11	2117.69	2054	63.58
18	4/27/15	2119.29	2108.29	2089	19.00
19	5/4/15	2110.23	2116.10	2080	35.87
20	5/11/15	2115.56	2122.73	2086	37.17
21	5/18/15	2121.30	2126.06	2091	34.76
22	5/25/15	2125.34	2107.39	2095	12.05
23	6/1/15	2108.64	2092.83	2079	14.19
24	6/8/15	2092.34	2094.11	2062	31.77
25	6/15/15	2091.34	2109.99	2061	48.65
26	6/22/15	2112.50	2101.49	2083	18.99
27	6/29/15	2098.63	2076.78	2069	8.15
28	7/6/15	2073.95	2076.62	2044	32.67
29	7/13/15	2080.03	2126.64	2050	76.61
30	7/20/15	2126.85	2079.65	2097	-17.20
31	7/27/15	2078.19	2103.84	2048	55.65
32	8/3/15	2104.49	2077.57	2074	3.08
33	8/10/15	2080.98	2091.54	2051	40.56
34	8/17/15	2089.70	1970.89	2060	-88.81
35	8/24/15	1965.15	1988.87	1935	53.72
36	8/31/15	1986.73	1921.22	1957	-35.51
37	9/7/15	1927.30	1961.05	1897	63.75
38	9/14/15	1963.06	1958.03	1933	24.97
39	9/21/15	1960.84	1931.34	1930	1.34
40	9/28/15	1929.18	1951.36	1899	52.18
41	10/5/15	1954.33	2014.89	1924	90.56
42	10/12/15	2015.65	2033.11	1986	47.46
43	10/19/15	2031.73	2075.15	2002	73.42
44	10/26/15	2075.08	2079.36	2045	34.28
45	11/2/15	2080.76	2099.20	2051	48.44
46	11/9/15	2096.56	2023.04	2067	-43.52
47	11/16/15	2022.08	2089.17	1992	97.09
48	11/23/15	2089.41	2090.11	2059	30.70
49	11/30/15	2090.95	2091.69	2061	30.74
50	12/7/15	2090.42	2012.37	2060	-48.05
51	12/14/15	2013.37	2005.55	1983	22.18
52	12/21/15	2010.27	2060.99	1980	80.72
53	12/28/15	2057.77	2043.94	2028	16.17

Year 2014

Week	Date	Open	Close	Put Sold	Outcome
1	12/30/13	1841.47	1831.37	1811	19.90
2	1/6/14	1832.31	1842.37	1802	40.06
3	1/13/14	1841.26	1838.70	1811	27.44
4	1/20/14	1841.05	1790.29	1811	-20.76
5	**1/27/14**	1791.03	1782.59	1761	21.56
6	2/3/14	1782.68	1797.02	1753	44.34
7	2/10/14	1796.20	1838.63	1766	72.43
8	2/17/14	1839.03	1836.25	1809	27.22
9	2/24/14	1836.78	1859.45	1807	52.67
10	3/3/14	1857.68	1878.04	1828	50.36
11	3/10/14	1877.86	1841.13	1850	-8.87
12	3/17/14	1842.81	1866.52	1813	53.71
13	3/24/14	1867.67	1857.62	1838	19.95
14	3/31/14	1859.16	1865.09	1829	35.93
15	4/7/14	1863.92	1815.69	1834	-18.23
16	**4/14/14**	1818.18	1864.85	1788	76.67
17	4/21/14	1865.79	1863.40	1836	27.61
18	4/28/14	1865.00	1881.14	1835	46.14
19	5/5/14	1879.45	1878.48	1849	29.03
20	5/12/14	1880.03	1877.86	1850	27.83
21	5/19/14	1876.66	1900.53	1847	53.87
22	5/26/14	1902.01	1923.57	1872	51.56
23	6/2/14	1923.87	1949.44	1894	55.57
24	6/9/14	1948.97	1936.16	1919	17.19
25	6/16/14	1934.84	1962.87	1905	58.03
26	6/23/14	1962.92	1960.96	1933	28.04
27	6/30/14	1960.79	1985.44	1931	54.65
28	7/7/14	1984.22	1967.57	1954	13.35
29	7/14/14	1969.86	1978.22	1940	38.36
30	7/21/14	1976.93	1978.34	1947	31.41
31	7/28/14	1978.25	1925.15	1948	-23.10
32	**8/4/14**	1926.62	1931.59	1897	34.97
33	8/11/14	1933.43	1955.06	1903	51.63
34	8/18/14	1958.36	1988.40	1928	60.04
35	8/25/14	1991.74	2003.37	1962	41.63
36	9/1/14	2004.07	2007.71	1974	33.64
37	9/8/14	2007.17	1985.54	1977	8.37
38	9/15/14	1986.04	2010.40	1956	54.36
39	9/22/14	2009.08	1982.85	1980	2.85
40	9/29/14	1978.96	1967.90	1949	18.94
41	10/6/14	1970.01	1906.13	1940	-33.88
42	**10/13/14**	1905.65	1886.76	1876	11.11
43	**10/20/14**	1885.62	1964.58	1856	108.96
44	10/27/14	1962.97	2018.05	1933	85.08
45	11/3/14	2018.21	2031.92	1988	43.71
46	11/10/14	2032.01	2039.82	2002	37.81
47	11/17/14	2038.29	2063.50	2008	55.21
48	11/24/14	2065.07	2067.56	2035	32.49
49	12/1/14	2065.78	2075.37	2036	39.59
50	12/8/14	2074.84	2002.33	2045	-42.51
51	**12/15/14**	2005.03	2070.65	1975	95.62
52	12/22/14	2069.28	2088.77	2039	49.49
53	12/29/14	2087.63	2058.90	2060	-1.10